Samuel French Acting Edition

I Can't Keep Running in Place

by Barbara Schottenfeld

‖SAMUEL FRENCH‖

Copyright © 1979 (under the title *A Woman Suspended*)
by Barbara Schottenfeld
Copyright © 1980 by Barbara Schottenfeld
Copyright © 1981 for the song "What If We" by Barbara Schottenfeld
Copyright © 1982 by Barbara Schottenfeld
All Rights Reserved

I CAN'T KEEP RUNNING IN PLACE is fully protected under the copyright laws of the United States of America, the British Commonwealth, including Canada, and all member countries of the Berne Convention for the Protection of Literary and Artistic Works, the Universal Copyright Convention, and/or the World Trade Organization conforming to the Agreement on Trade Related Aspects of Intellectual Property Rights. All rights, including professional and amateur stage productions, recitation, lecturing, public reading, motion picture, radio broadcasting, television, online/digital production, and the rights of translation into foreign languages are strictly reserved.

ISBN 978-0-573-68121-9

www.concordtheatricals.com
www.concordtheatricals.co.uk

FOR PRODUCTION INQUIRIES
UNITED STATES AND CANADA
info@concordtheatricals.com
1-866-979-0447

UNITED KINGDOM AND EUROPE
licensing@concordtheatricals.co.uk
020-7054-7200

Each title is subject to availability from Concord Theatricals Corp., depending upon country of performance. Please be aware that *I CAN'T KEEP RUNNING IN PLACE* may not be licensed by Concord Theatricals Corp. in your territory. Professional and amateur producers should contact the nearest Concord Theatricals Corp. office or licensing partner to verify availability.

CAUTION: Professional and amateur producers are hereby warned that *I CAN'T KEEP RUNNING IN PLACE* is subject to a licensing fee. The purchase, renting, lending or use of this book does not constitute a license to perform this title(s), which license must be obtained from Concord Theatricals Corp. prior to any performance. Performance of this title(s) without a license is a violation of federal law and may subject the producer and/or presenter of such performances to civil penalties. Both amateurs and professionals considering a production are strongly advised to apply to the appropriate agent before starting rehearsals, advertising, or booking a theatre.

Please refer to page 87 for further copyright information.

For my father, Milton,
my mother, Mina,
and my brother, Steven.

WESTSIDE ARTS THEATRE
(CHERYL CRAWFORD THEATRE)

RAY GASPARD
in association with
CHRIS SILVA, STEPHEN DAILEY and **WILL DAILEY**
present

I CAN'T KEEP RUNNING IN PLACE
a new musical

Book, Music and Lyrics by
BARBARA SCHOTTENFELD

Starring
MARCIA RODD

with

| EVALYN BARON | MARY DONNET | JOY FRANZ | BEV LARSON | JENNIE VENTRISS |

And Also Starring

HELEN GALLAGHER

| *Set Design by* | *Costume Design by* | *Lighting Design by* |
| **URSULA BELDEN** | **CHRISTINA WEPPNER** | **VICTOR EN YU TAN** |

| *Choreographed by* | *Musical Supervision* | *Musical Director* |
| **BAAYORK LEE** | **JOHN McKINNEY** | **ROBERT HIRSCHHORN** |

| *Assistant Choreographer* | *Orchestrations by* |
| **DENNIS GRIMALDI** | **BARBARA SCHOTTENFELD** |

| *Casting by* | *Production Stage Manager* |
| **JUDY COURTNEY, BCI** | **MERYL SCHAFFER** |

Directed by
SUSAN EINHORN

I CAN'T KEEP RUNNING IN PLACE was produced by Ray Gaspard in association with Chris Silva, Stephen Dailey and Will Dailey at the Westside Arts Theatre in New York, on May 14, 1981, with the following cast:

Michelle	MARCIA RODD
Beth	HELEN GALLAGHER
Eileen	JOY FRANZ
Alice	EVALYN BARON
Sherry	BEV LARSON
Mandy	MARY DONNET
Gwen	JENNIE VENTRISS

Director: Susan Einhorn
Choreographer: Baayork Lee
Set Design: Ursula Belden
Lighting Design: Victor En Yu Tan
Costume Design: Christina Weppner
Production Stage Manager: Meryl Schaffer
Vocal and Orchestral Arrangements: Barbara Schottenfeld
Musical Director: Robert Hirschhorn
Musical Supervisor: John McKinney
Casting by: Judy Courtney, B.C.I.
Press Representative: Jeff Richards

"I CAN'T KEEP RUNNING IN PLACE" was given its first New York production by Ellen Stewart at La Mama E.T.C. in February, 1980. The cast included Melinda Tanner, Catherine Wolf, Suellen Estey, Maggie Anderson, Bev Larson, Eva Charney, and Annie Korzen. The production was directed by Susan Einhorn with musical direction by Robert Hirschhorn.

The play was previously produced at Princeton University under the title "A WOMAN SUSPENDED." The cast included Petie Duncan, Dorothy Edwards, Carol V. Elliott, Nancy J. Newman, Cheryl Chang, Karen Lee Hertz, Bernice Hicks, and Jan Maxwell. The production was directed by the author.

MUSICAL NUMBERS

ACT I

"I'M GLAD I'M HERE"	The Company	11
"DON'T SAY YES IF YOU WANT TO SAY NO"	Michelle and Company	16
"I CAN'T KEEP RUNNING IN PLACE"	Eileen	24
"I'M ON MY OWN"	Michelle	26
"MORE OF ME TO LOVE"	Gwen and Alice	33
"I LIVE ALONE"	Beth	38
"I CAN COUNT ON YOU"	Alice and Company	42

ACT II

"PENIS ENVY"	Michelle and Company	51
"GET THE ANSWER NOW"	Sherry and Company	57
"WHAT IF WE . . ."	Michelle	63
"ALMOSTS, MAYBES AND PERHAPSES"	Beth	68
"WHERE WILL I BE NEXT WEDNESDAY NIGHT?"	The Company	76

CHARACTERS

The cast is comprised of seven women in an assertiveness training workshop, led by a psychologist, Michelle. The participants are: Gwen, Beth, Eileen, Alice, Sherry, and Mandy.

MICHELLE — Late 30's. The psychologist leading the workshop. Dynamic and sensitive.

BETH — Mid 40's. Funny, bitchy, bitter. Rich suburban housewife.

GWEN — Early to mid 40's. Overweight, housewife-mother.

EILEEN — Early 30's. About 4 months pregnant with her fifth child. Wants to go back to school.

SHERRY — Mid 20's. Working girl. Health food fanatic. Over-enthusiastic about everything.

ALICE — Mid 20's. Very overweight, an actress, always the comedienne.

MANDY — Early 20's. Sarah Lawrence student, pre-med, spoiled.

SETTING

A workshop space in Michelle's Soho loft. The set is primarily decorated with plants and should give a feeling of simplicity and spaciousness. The furniture is movable and adaptable.

Up stage left is the entry way. There is another area on the side, which leads to the main part of Michelle's loft. This side area contains a desk with a telephone. The women can hear any conversation that might occur in the side area, given its proximity to the workshop space.

SCENES

The workshop takes place over the course of six Wednesday night sessions, from late winter to early spring.

ACT ONE

SCENE 1 — The first session
SCENE 2 — Later that night
SCENE 3 — The third session

ACT TWO

SCENE 1 — The fifth session
SCENE 2 — The sixth and last session

EXPLANATION OF ROLE-PLAYING

Role-playing is used in both comic and serious scenes in the play. Behavioral psychologists believe that one of the most effective ways of making the transition from the discussion of a conflict to taking action on the problem is through role-playing the conflict with another member of the group. The idea is that by first exploring and then rehearsing a desired behavior, one can then "perform" the newly-acquired attitude in transactions in the real-life situations.

For instance, when Eileen is acting out a personal conflict, another woman in the group will assume the role of Eileen's husband or Eileen herself. When Michelle gets an insight into Eileen's feelings, Michelle gets up from her seat and stands behind Eileen. Eileen will stop speaking and allow Michelle to speak for her as an "alter-ego." Other women may simultaneously serve as such alter-egos; within one scene, several women may play Eileen and/or Eileen's husband, giving Eileen potential insights into her conflict.

I Can't Keep Running In Place

ACT ONE

SCENE 1

THE FIRST SESSION

Music begins in blackout. The first scene begins in darkness with isolated lighting on EACH WOMAN *who speaks or sings at a particular moment. Only* MICHELLE *remains unlit when* SHE *is speaking.*

MICHELLE'S VOICE. Now I want you to feel all the tension of your whole body in your right arm. Tight. Tight. Tighter aaaaand drop it. (*Sound of arms hitting the floor, exhalations.*) Now, tense your whole body. Tense your right arm, then your left, right leg, left leg, calves, thighs, pelvis, waist, chest, shoulders, neck muscles, scrunch your face up tight, tighter, tighterrrr, lift up aaand release. (*Sounds of exhaustion and exhalation.*) Good. Now I'm going to keep the lights dim a little bit longer. Just relax. Clear your head of any tension in whatever way works best for you. You may want to imagine you're lying back in a hot, soothing bath after a tiring day. Feel the hot water looooosening your muscles. Or this works really well when you're trying to get those lower back muscles against the floor ... Imagine you are a Hershey Bar melting onto the sidewalk with the sun directly overhead. SSSSSSSmush... (*Light flashes on* BETH.)

BETH. (*Sarcastically.*) Lovely! (*MUSIC begins.*)

MICHELLE'S VOICE.... and you're melting deeper and deeper into the crevices of the sidewalk until all of your muscles feel soft and gooey ... (*Light on* MANDY.)

MANDY.
WHAT DOES HERSHEYS HAVE TO DO WITH ASSERTIVENESS TRAINING?

MICHELLE'S VOICE.... and you can feel your whole body sinking into the pavement ... (*Light on* EILEEN.)

EILEEN.
WHY IS "RELAXING" MAKING ME TENSE?
MICHELLE. Smush . . . Smush . . . (*Light on* GWEN.)
GWEN.
WELL, AT LEAST I'M NOT HOME WHERE EVERYBODY'S COMPLAINING . . .
MICHELLE'S VOICE. . . . looooooooooooooooooooosening eeeeeeeeeeeeeeeeeverything. (*Light on* BETH.)
BETH.
IF I LEFT RIGHT NOW,
I WONDER IF THIS MICHELLE WOULD TAKE OFFENSE? (*Light on* EILEEN.)
EILEEN.
THIS RELAXING IS KILLING ME. (*Lights up.*)
MICHELLE. Okay. Would you all please get up? I want to do an exercise where you create a machine, any kind of machine. One person starts and then each of you will join in and become a part of it. Can I have a volunteer?
BETH.
WHY DID I DECIDE TO COME?
GWEN.
INSIDE I'M NUMB . . .
MANDY.
MY HANDS ARE FROZEN . . .
EILEEN.
MY PALMS ARE SWEATY . . .
SHERRY.
I'M NOT FEELING VERY COMFORTABLE . . .
ALICE.
I'LL KILL THAT NANCY ROSEN . . .
BETH.
GOD! IS THIS DUMB!
ALICE.
WHY DID SHE STICK HER NOSE IN . . .
BETH.
I KNOW I OUGHT TO STAY BUT I'M NOT GOING TO . . .
ALICE.
SHE SAID THIS WEDNESDAY NIGHT GROUP
WOULD BE A GOOD THING FOR US TO JOIN!
MANDY.
I REGRET THIS ALREADY . . .

MICHELLE. (*Motioning to begin.*) Okay.
GWEN.
I SHOULD HAVE REALIZED I'D FEEL GUILTY . . .
BETH.
I'M GOING HOME . . .
GWEN.
FOR LEAVING JEROME . . .
BETH.
JUST AS SOON AS I CAN DO IT SOMEWHAT GRACEFULLY.
GWEN.
BY HIMSELF WITH THE KIDS . . .
ALICE.
I DON'T SEE YOU, NANCY ROSEN,
WHERE ARE YOU, NANCY ROSEN?
SHERRY.
I'M NOT FEELING VERY COMFORTABLE . . .
ALICE.
WHERE ARE YOU, NANCY?
ALL.
BUT I'M GLAD I'M HERE,
I'M GLAD I'M HERE.
I'M GLAD I'M HERE,

YES, I'M GLAD I'M HERE,
I'M GLAD I'M HERE,
I'M GLAD I'M HERE.

IF I'M FORTY-TWO (*Each woman says her age.*)
AND I DON'T KNOW WHO I AM,
WHAT'S A SIX-WEEK CRASH COURSE GOING TO SHOW ME?
IF I TELL THESE STRANGERS MY PROBLEMS,
WHY SHOULD THEY GIVE A DAMN?
AND I'M NOT SURE I REALLY WANT THEM TO KNOW ME.
MANDY.
I WISH I'D KNOWN MORE ABOUT THIS . . .
BEFORE I MADE MY MIND UP.
EILEEN.
BEFORE I PAID AND SIGNED UP
FOR ALL SIX SESSIONS.

GWEN.
IT'S THAT WEIRD KIND OF WORKSHOP!
MANDY.
WELL, THIS LOOKS LIKE A "WHAT'S YOUR QUIRK-SHOP"
WHERE YOU LOOK INTO YOUR PAST WITH A TELESCOPE,
AND MAKE CONFESSIONS.
MICHELLE. Good. Now would you all please form a semicircle around me? We are going to do what's called a trust exercise. Just watch me and catch me when I fall, then each of you will do the same (*She falls.*)
ALL.
YES, I'M GLAD I'M HERE,
BUT I'M ALSO AFRAID,
IS THAT A VERY ABNORMAL REACTION? (SHERRY *falls.*)
ALL THESE FACES I SEE
THEY'RE JUST WOMEN LIKE ME,
SO WHY IS MY HEART BEAT IN TRACTION? (ALICE *falls, hitting floor.*)
OH OH OH AH!
SO SO SO SAH!
NICE TO LA LA MEET BLAH!
DON'T I KNOW YA YA FROM THE
(*Pointing to* EILEEN.) P.T.A.,
(*Pointing to* GWEN.) U.J.A.,
(*Pointing to* SHERRY.) E.S.T.
BETH.
OR S.O.B.?
ALL.
BEE BEE BEE DO!
SEE SEE SEE SO!
WHAT A LOVELY FA FA BEE WAH. (BETH *falls.*)
JA JA JA, GA GA, BA RA . . .
PEE DEE REE, BO BO TOE . . .
TAY TAY TAY, WELL, LA NA NA (EILEEN *falls.*)
NA NA NA NA-ICE (*Nice.*) TO LA LA MEET BLAH.

I'M QUITE SINCERE
I'M GLAD I'M HERE,
I'M GLAD I'M HERE.

YES, I'M GLAD I'M HERE.
I'M GLAD I'M HERE.
YES, GLAD I'M HERE! (GWEN *hesitates and finally falls, ending on final beat.*)

(*For the following introductions, the staging should suggest that* THE WOMEN *are seated in a circle.* EACH WOMAN *faces a different part of the audience at a strong angle, always looking straight ahead.* EACH *listens to the present speaker without looking at her. If possible, the lighting should be a strong spot from above which shifts with each new speaker, which will heighten the stylized quality of the scene. The speeches must overlap exactly; so that each speech is linked to the next by a common word or phrase which is spoken by two women at the exact same time. Following the overlap at the end of her introduction,* EACH WOMAN *lowers the volume of her voice for the remainder of the speech and then silently mouths an additional sentence or two.*)

MICHELLE. Thank you, find a seat please. Now, to begin with, I want to welcome you to the first session of the Women's Assertiveness Training Workshop. What I would like each of us to do is to tell each other something about ourselves. My name is Michelle Bennet. A few years ago I went back to school for my degree in Psychology. I have two children, Ellen, age fourteen, and Russell, age nine. My husband and I separated five months ago. I am active and assertive, and I feel in control of my life which is SOMETHING I value more than anything . . .

GWEN. SOMETHING about myself. Well, I'm Gwen. I got married young and still am, married, that is, and I'm glad to be. I have three children whom I love very much. And I have a husband, OF COURSE . . .

BETH. (*Coolly.*) OF COURSE, when I feel like talking about myself, I will. But I have to feel like it. I just can't do it at gunpoint. I hope that's ALL RIGHT . . .

SHERRY. (*Quickly, with abundant energy.*) ALL RIGHT. Let's see. My name is Sherry and I'm twenty-six. I mean, twenty-seven, and I'm really a lot brighter than I sound. I am very happy all the time, or very happy most of the time and pretty happy the remainder of the time. I'm a happy person. I'm a Pisces. I work in a boutique. My hobbies are meditation and tap dancing. I'm living with a guy I like a whole lot and I really want to get married. The kind of guy I'VE ALWAYS LOVED is very, very . . .

ALICE. I'VE ALWAYS LOVED performing, my first major success being Miss Junior Jerseyette in Atlantic City at age five. My name is Alice Robbins. That's my stage name, in case you're wondering why it's Robbins when my face screams Rabinowitz. I'm not considering committing marriage. Uh . . . AT THE MOMENT I'm not performing . . .

MICHELLE. AT THE MOMENT I am at Sarah Lawrence, but I'll be at Yale Medical School next fall. Right now I'm studying Psych (that's Psychology). And that is why I am in the workshop. As an observer. Not as a participant. I mean, I paid my money and I am allowed to participate, but I'd prefer to keep that to a minimum since I don't have any major problems, and it wouldn't be fair to use up your time. I am writing my thesis on The Assertiveness Training Workshop as a Socio-psychological Phenomenon of the Eighties. When I discussed it with my advisor, Marshall Herbert, I'm sure you've heard of him . . . Anyway, WE HAD decided . . .

EILEEN. WE HAD our first child to prove to our friends that we were normal. We had the second to keep the first one company. We had the third so that the first two would not compete. Etc., Etc. (EILEEN *puts up another finger when each new child is mentioned, as if counting to four on one hand. On the second "Etc." she merely touches her stomach.*)

(*MUSIC BEGINS IMMEDIATELY.*)

SONG: *"DON'T SAY YES IF YOU WANT TO SAY NO"*

MICHELLE. (*Spoken over vamp.*) Now, I want you to think of a time when you did not say no and ended up doing something you did not want to do. (EACH WOMAN, *except* MANDY, *quickly selects a place on the Stage where* SHE *can recreate her particular predicament.*) Imagine everything you can about that situation. Mandy, please participate. (MANDY *shakes her head no.*) O.K. Where are you?

ALICE.
I'M AT THE MOVIES.
I LOVE THE MOVIES.
I'M WATCHING JOHN WAYNE.

I HATE JOHN WAYNE.
IT'S A WESTERN,
I HATE WESTERNS.

I WAS IN THE MOOD TO SEE A FELLINI,
BERTOLUCCI, BUNUEL, OR EVEN TRUFFAUT,
BUT HE SUGGESTED JOHN WAYNE OR ELSE "THE GENITAL GENIE,"
I DID NOT WANT TO GO, BUT I DID NOT KNOW HOW TO SAY NO.
   MICHELLE.
DON'T SAY YES IF YOU WANT TO SAY NO,
DON'T AGREE JUST BECAUSE HE'S YOUR BEAU,
DON'T CALL IT A SPADE IF YOU KNOW IT'S A HOE,
DON'T SAY YES IF YOU WANT TO SAY NO.
   SHERRY.
I'M IN BED WITH A GUY AND WE'RE TRYING TO MAKE IT.
HE IS STUPID, UNATTRACTIVE, HE LISPS, AND HE'S SLOW,
AND THAT'S WHEN HE'S DRESSED;
YOU SHOULD SEE HIM STARK NAKED!
AND ALL BECAUSE I COULDN'T SAY NO.
   MICHELLE.
DON'T SAY YES IF YOU WANT TO SAY NO,
DON'T UNDRESS IF YOU'RE CON AND HE'S PRO,
YET DON'T SAY STOP IF YOU WANT TO SAY GO,
DON'T SAY YES IF YOU WANT TO SAY NO.

SAY WHAT YOU MEAN
THERE'S NO IN-BETWEEN,
MAYBES ARE LIKE RABIES,
IT'S NOT SOMETHING YOU WANT, SO
LISTEN TO THE CURING STUFF:
DON'T BE DEMURE, BE TOUGH!
YOU MUST BE SECURE ENOUGH
TO RISK NOT BEING NICE.
ONE LITTLE WORD WILL SUFFICE,
AND THAT LITTLE WORD IS N . . .
   GWEN.
YES, YES, YES,
ALTHOUGH SHE REALLY NEEDS THAT OINTMENT,

MOMMY WILL CANCEL HER APPOINTMENT,
IN ORDER TO GIVE YOU A RIDE TO THE POOL.
   Eileen.
I REALLY DON'T THINK THAT
ALL MY SAVINGS SHOULD GO INTO A JOINT ACCOUNT.
WELL, WHAT CAN I SAY?
WELL THEN, HAVE IT YOUR WAY, O.K.
   Beth.
BUT I DON'T NEED ANOTHER SET OF ENCYCLOPEDIA
BRITTANICA . . .
I ALREADY HAVE TWO . . .
WILL A MONEY ORDER DO?
   Sherry.
I REALLY DON'T WANT TO
'CAUSE WE DON'T HAVE PROTECTION . . .
IT'S REALLY NOT THAT I'M BEING SELFISH
IT'S JUST THAT I . . .
OH PLEASE DON'T MAKE ME FEEL GUILTY,
IT'S JUST THAT I . . .
(*Suddenly opens legs.*)
ALL RIGHT, ALL RIGHT, LET'S DO IT,
ALL RIGHT, ALL RIGHT, LET'S GO THROUGH IT,
QUICKLY! I'LL JUST PRAY . . . A LOT!

(The Women *continue to sing about their respective problems in musical counterpoint while* Michelle *goes to* Each Woman *and instructs her to say "NO." The* Women *then replace the words of their previous remarks with "NO," which* They *sing repeatedly to the same counterpoint melodies. The* Women *continue to sing "NO" as* They *form a circle around* Michelle *and sing the following in triumph:*)

   All except Mandy.
IT FEELS SO GOOD TO SAY NO, NO, NO.
I REALLY SHOULD LEARN TO SAY NO, NO, NO.
OH THE KINETIC FLOW, FLOW, FLOW
OF THAT POETIC NO, NO, NO.
   Michelle.
SAY IT LOUDLY!
   All.
SAY IT PROUDLY!
TO YOUR BEST FRIEND

OR YOUR WORST FOE, FOE, FOE.
MICHELLE.
WITH STACCATO
ALL EXCEPT MANDY.
(*NO! NO! NO!*)
MICHELLE.
WITH VIBRATO
ALL EXCEPT MANDY. (*With exaggerated vibrato.*)
(NOOOO, NOOOOO, NOOOO . . .)
MICHELLE.
BUT DON'T FORGET THE MOTTO:
ALL EXCEPT MANDY.
DON'T SAY YES IF YOU WANT TO SAY
NO, NO, NO. NO, NO, NO. NO, NO, NO. NO, NO, NO.
NO, NO, NO. NO, NO, NO. NO, NO, NO, *NOOOO!*

(*As the music becomes increasingly jazzy, the* WOMEN *form a kickline.* THEY *are aware of the irony.*)

ALL EXCEPT MANDY. (*Continued.*)
DON'T SAY YES IF YOU WANT TO SAY NO!
(*Spoken.*) No!

MICHELLE. Everyone get comfortable. I want to begin the last part of the session with a discussion. I'd like to hear what your families said about your taking this workshop.
GWEN. I still haven't mentioned it.
EILEEN. I did.
GWEN. I sure didn't. My husband thinks I'm at a P.T.A. meeting, making up safety patrol zones and voting on chaperoning at the eighth grade prom.
MICHELLE. Why don't you want to tell him?
GWEN. Are you kidding? If my husband knew I was spending his hard-earned money learning to become a Hershey Bar taking a bath . . .
ALICE. An assertive Hershey Bar!
MICHELLE. What I'd like each of us to do is . . .
BETH. Be an Almond Joy in a sauna.
MICHELLE. No. Not exactly. Eileen, what did you tell your husband about the workshop and what was his reaction?
EILEEN. I told him it was a workshop for women which teaches women to be strong, I guess, and to say what you're feel-

ing and to consider your own feelings important . . . what else . . . whatever it said in the ad I saw.

MICHELLE. And what did *he* say?

EILEEN. Well, I asked him if he would mind my taking the workshop, especially since it meant my being out an evening during the week, which I know he doesn't like.

MICHELLE. He's usually home at night during the week?

EILEEN. No. He has business meetings and things, but that changes all the time. What I mean is, he never knows until that day if there is going to be a meeting and he likes to know that when he does come home that I'll be there.

MICHELLE. Is that fair?

EILEEN. It's just the way it's always been.

MICHELLE. Well, what did he say?

EILEEN. Well, at first he didn't really agree or disagree, he just shrugged his shoulders.

GWEN. Oh, does yours do that too? I guess they all come with the shoulder shrug.

MICHELLE. You were saying, Eileen?

EILEEN. He just shrugged and said, "You don't care what I think anyway, so do what you want."

MICHELLE. What's your husband's name?

EILEEN. John.

MICHELLE. O.K. Who wants to start out playing John? (SHERRY *waves hand.*) Sherry?

SHERRY. I did role-playing in my psychodrama group. And anyway, in school plays I always played the villain.

EILEEN. He's not a villain!

SHERRY. Hey, I'm sorry. Just kidding.

EILEEN. No, I'm sorry. I didn't mean to . . .

MICHELLE. To say what you mean?

EILEEN. No, I didn't mean to be so curt.

SHERRY. You weren't curt.

EILEEN. I wasn't?

MICHELLE. Not at all. You were direct.

EILEEN. I was? But I thought I was defensive.

MICHELLE. You weren't defensive. You came to your defense. There's a difference.

EILEEN. Hm?

MICHELLE. If a man says what he means, he's direct. If a woman says what she means, she's curt.

BETH. (*Dryly.*) Or she lacks tact.

EILEEN. (*To* MICHELLE.) You're right. I shouldn't have apologized. I'm sorry I ap— (WOMEN *laugh.*)

I CAN'T KEEP RUNNING IN PLACE

SHERRY. O.K. (EILEEN *and* SHERRY *cross down into role-playing area.*) Let's see, he said something like "You don't really care what I think anyway, so do whatever you want," right?

EILEEN. Yeah, that's close enough. (*To* MICHELLE.) Then I asked him what he meant by that.

MICHELLE. All right then, ask him. (*Gesturing towards* SHERRY.)

EILEEN. What do you mean?

SHERRY. (*John.*) (*Tough "macho" accent, like Stanley Kowalski.*) You know what I'm talking about, Eileen. So what if I did object to your taking this course, being out at night, would that really stop you?

EILEEN. (*Taken aback by* SHERRY'*s characterization.*) Yes. (*Pause.*) I mean, it might.

SHERRY. (*John.*) It might! You mean, if I mildly object, you may be willing to give it up, but if I tell you I'm really against it, then you'll absolutely go.

EILEEN. That's ridiculous.

SHERRY. (*John.*) Have you forgotten you're pregnant?

EILEEN. No, John.

SHERRY. (*John.*) Then act pregnant. (*The* WOMEN *are amused by* SHERRY'*s portrayal of* JOHN.) I'd like to know when all this is going to end.

EILEEN. What? When is what going to end?

SHERRY. This charade you're playing. Two words, three syllables. Women's lib. Look at me, everybody, I'm a Women's Libber. I do what I damn well please and you can't do a thing about it.

EILEEN. (*Crossing away from* "JOHN") Then I left the room. (SHERRY *takes her seat.*)

MICHELLE. Why?

EILEEN. Because he uses that Women's Lib line to antagonize me. I'm not even part of that whole "Women's Lib" feminist thing.

MICHELLE. Any other reason?

EILEEN. I was afraid to discuss it any more.

MICHELLE. Why?

EILEEN. I know if I stayed he would have told me he loves me.

SHERRY. So what's wrong with that?

EILEEN. He makes me feel guilty.

MICHELLE. How?

EILEEN. Because he accuses me of changing, and of wanting something he can't give me anymore.

MICHELLE. And then he tells you he loves you?

EILEEN. Right. And that he needs me.
MANDY. Don't you think this is a little ridiculous?
MICHELLE. What do you mean?
MANDY. Jesus. Where have you been?
EILEEN. I don't understand . . .
MICHELLE. Let's finish the scene.
EILEEN. I told you, that's all there was.
MICHELLE. I know, but see what happens if John uses the "I love you" compassion-trap techique. But don't let him manipulate you.
ALICE. (*Mock-sexy.*) Why not? (MICHELLE *gestures to role-playing area.*)
EILEEN. All right, I'll give it a try. Oh, and Sherry, John doesn't talk like that.
SHERRY. Oh, sure. Sorry. (*From now on,* SHERRY *attempts to play John in a less caricatured manner, yet still tries to be masculine.*) Like, I want to still love you, but you won't let me. You're changing, Eileen. You're moving away from me. I barely recognize you.
MICHELLE. (*As Eileen.*) Then look harder, John.
SHERRY. (*John.*) You're getting to be so . . .
MICHELLE. (*As Eileen.*) Confident? Independent? (*Urges others to participate; each woman stands up on her line.*)
ALICE. Thinking? (MICHELLE *urges, but they hesitate.*)
MICHELLE. Restless?
SHERRY. (*John.*) No. Strong. Aggressive. Unsympathetic.
MICHELLE. (*As John.*) You think about yourself first.
BETH. (*As John.*) You care about your own feelings first.
GWEN. (*As John.*) You place your happiness above mine and the children's.
MANDY. Give me a break. (*From this point on, the* WOMEN *are always speaking as* JOHN.)
MICHELLE. You're getting selfish.
SHERRY. Defiant.
ALICE. Strong.
MICHELLE. Selfish.
SHERRY. Defiant.
ALICE. Strong. (*The* WOMEN *begin to encircle* EILEEN.)
MICHELLE. Who is this stranger?
BETH. Who is this stranger?
MICHELLE. You know I need you. (*Tries to involve* MANDY, *who resists; moves to* GWEN.)

GWEN. You know I need you.
MICHELLE. I thought you loved me.
ALICE. I thought you loved me.
MICHELLE. Could I be wrong?
SHERRY. Could I be wrong?
MICHELLE. You're getting selfish!
SHERRY. You're getting selfish!
BETH. Self-seeking.
ALICE. Defiant.
GWEN. And strong.
SHERRY. Selfish!
BETH. Self-seeking.
ALICE. Defiant.
GWEN. And strong.
MICHELLE. You're doing this to test your power.
ALICE. You're doing this to prove a point.
GWEN. I'm warning you.
BETH. You'll be sorry.
MICHELLE. (*As Eileen.*) (*Crossing to* EILEEN.) I'm not doing this to test my power. I'm not doing this to prove a point. I want you to understand how I feel.
EILEEN. (*Hesitantly.*) John, do you know what it's like to be with four children all the time and to . . .
ALICE. Come to bed, come to bed . . .
EILEEN. John, I'm frustrated and I'm . . .
ALICE. You're overtired. We'll make love, satisfaction guaranteed.
EILEEN. I don't want you to feel threatened, but . . .
BETH. I'm not threatened, not at all. In fact, you're cuter when you're tough.
GWEN. Why do you want to go to school, when there are plenty of books in this house you've never read?
SHERRY. Where is the person I married?
EILEEN. I'm not the exact same person you married.
SHERRY. You're betraying me by changing.
EILEEN. I don't understand what you mean.
SHERRY. Did I ever hurt you?
EILEEN. (*Softly.*) No.
ALICE. Did I ever leave you?
EILEEN. No. (*The tempo continues to accelerate.*)
MICHELLE. (*As Eileen.*) No, but you've taken some part of me.

EILEEN. You've taken some part of me.
MICHELLE. (*As Eileen.*) And I want it back.
EILEEN. And I want it back.
MICHELLE. (*As Eileen.*) I've got different needs now,
EILEEN. I've got different needs now,
MICHELLE. (*As Eileen.*) There's something out there I've got to find,
EILEEN. There's something I've got to find.
MICHELLE. (*As Eileen.*) I need to change.
EILEEN. I need to change.
SHERRY. (*As John.*) And it's a woman's prerogative to change her mind?
EILEEN. Don't mock me.
ALICE. (*As John.*) I love you.
EILEEN. (*Exploding.*) Don't! Please don't do that!

"I CAN'T KEEP RUNNING IN PLACE"
("LET ME CHANGE")

LET ME CHANGE . . .

I CAN'T KEEP RUNNING IN PLACE,
IT'S TIME I ENTERED THE RACE,
THIS WORLD'S TOO SWEET TO RESIST,
I WANT TO LIVE, NOT JUST EXIST.

LET ME CHANGE, LET ME CHANGE . . .

I'M IN A COCOON BUT I'M FEELING MY WINGS,
I'D LIKE TO DO MAGNIFICENT THINGS,
THERE'S SOMEONE INSIDE ME THAT'S GOTTA GET LOOSE,
I'VE TRIED TO HIDE IT, BUT NOW IT'S NO USE.

LET ME CHANGE, LET ME CHANGE, LET ME CHANGE . . .

A CLOUD BECOMES A SHOWER,
AND RAIN TURNS TO SNOW,
A BLOSSOMING FLOWER
IS A TINY BUD THAT'S BEEN ALLOWED TO GROW.
SEASONS CHANGE

I CAN'T KEEP RUNNING IN PLACE

AND LEAVES TURN TO BLAZING RED,
ISN'T IT STRANGE
PEOPLE STAY THE SAME INSTEAD?

I CAN'T KEEP RUNNING IN PLACE,
IT'S TIME I ENTERED THE RACE,
THIS WORLD'S TOO SWEET TO RESIST,
I WANT TO LIVE,
I WANT TO LIVE . . .

THE SHAPE OF THE MOON IS DIFFERENT TONIGHT,
BUT IT STILL GIVES OFF LIGHT;
IT'S ONE OF THOSE BEAUTIFUL, CHANGING THINGS.

LET ME LEARN, LET ME GROW, LET ME CHANGE.
(*Song ends.*)
John, when we were first married you pleaded with me to stay in school and I was the one who wanted to start having babies and dinner parties and nervous breakdowns. I still love you. Differently than I used to, but I still really love you. I don't want to lose your love but I have to start respecting myself and my needs now. I am going to that workshop tonight and every Wednesday night for the next five weeks and I am also going back to school. (*No ONE speaks for several seconds. Laughs through tears, amazed.*) I did it! (*The* WOMEN *move to comfort her as LIGHTS FADE, "I CAN'T KEEP RUNNING IN PLACE" in background.* BETH *begins to move, but stops herself.* MICHELLE, MANDY, *and* BETH *look on as the others embrace* EILEEN.)

FADE TO BLACK

ACT ONE

SCENE 2

LATER THAT NIGHT.

MICHELLE. (*On phone.*) Heeeey! How's my favorite girl? I miss you, too, Sweetheart . . . (*Elated.*) He what? The lead? Well, Russell must be very excited. When is it? I'll fly up. Of course. Let me talk to Russell, honey . . . (*Matter-of-factly.*) Oh.

... Then put your fath ... Put Daddy on. (*Short pause.*) (*Coolly.*) Mark? How are you? Good. I'm fine. I mailed back your check again. I know it makes you feel better but I'm asking you not to. Fine. Can I talk to Russell? (*Pause.*) Russ? ... Are you on? ... Won't you say hello? Please? Surprise Mommy and say hello. (*Pause.*) Mommy called to talk to you. (*Pause.*) Congratulations, Sport. I want to come see you in the play ... and even if you're not sure right now, I want you to think about it ... Please say hello, Darling. Mommy wants to hear your pretty voice. (*Pause.*) I wish you wouldn't be angry with Mommy because you know she loves you and ... (RUSSELL *has hung up.* MICHELLE *remains by phone, deeply troubled. The phone rings.*) (*Happily.*) Russ? (*Suddenly stern.*) Well, what's going on? But he never acted like this before. Mark, he wouldn't talk to me! (*Slight pause.*) Okay ... (*With a new energy.*) Listen, how about if I come up for a few days? ... But maybe if I came up he'd ... Of course I remember it's your birthday. That's all the more reason the four of us should cele ... (*Suddenly angry.*) Fine. You don't want me there? *Good*! (SHE *slams down the phone.*)

(*MUSIC.*)

"I'M ON MY OWN"

MICHELLE.
HIS BIRTHDAY IS NEXT WEEK,
FORGETTING IT WON'T BE HARD,
I SPENT ALL OF YESTERDAY
NOT PICKING OUT A CARD.

I'M FREE TO SEE ANOTHER MAN,
OR TWO OR THREE OR MORE,
WHY DO I ACT LIKE POLLYANNA
WHEN WE GET TO THE DOOR?

NOW I CAN SLEEP AS LATE AS I LIKE,
WHY DO I STILL WAKE UP IN TIME TO FIX THEIR BREAKFAST AT EIGHT?
AT LAST I HAVE THE TIME TO READ EVERYTHING I

I CAN'T KEEP RUNNING IN PLACE

WANT TO,
WHY CAN'T I CONCENTRATE?

YES, I HAVE PEACE AND QUIET,
ALL DISTRACTION'S GONE,
WHY DO I ALWAYS KEEP THE RADIO ON?

THOSE WOMEN WOULD LOVE TO LEAD THE LIFE THAT I DO,
THEY THINK I'M HAPPY . . .
AND IT'S TRUE.

I'M ON MY OWN,
AND PROUD TO BE,
LIVING INDEPENDENTLY,
I'LL TAKE OUT AN AD SO HE CAN SEE,
I'M ON MY OWN.

SOON I WILL FORGET WITH EASE
OLD RESPONSIBILITIES,
WINTER COLDS AND SCRAPED-UP KNEES,
I'M ON MY OWN.

LOOK MA, NO HANDS,
I'LL CHEER MYSELF ON FROM THE STANDS,
I PASSED THE TEST, I'M FINALLY FREE,
PLEASE GIVE MY BEST TO THE OLD ME.

I SENT BACK MY SET OF KEYS,
NOW LIFE'S EASY, LIFE'S A BREEZE,
I DO ANYTHING I PLEASE,
I'M ON MY OWN.

I'M ON MY OWN,
AND FEELING FINE,
DREW MYSELF A NEW DESIGN.
MISTAKES I MAKE . . . I LOVE THEM . . . THEY'RE MINE,
I'M ON MY OWN.

LIKE A RUNNER ON THE TRACK,

READY, GET SET AND GO,
ONCE YOU START YOU DON'T LOOK BACK,
THAT'S ONE THING I KNOW.

I'M ON MY OWN,
AND PROUD TO BE
LIVING INDEPENDENTLY,
I'LL TAKE OUT AN AD SO HE CAN SEE,
I'M ON MY OWN.

I'M ON MY OWN,
MY HEAD IS CLEAR,
NO ONE'S HERE TO INTERFERE,
GOT MY SPACE, GOT MY CAREER,
I'M ON MY OWN. ON MY OWN.

I'M WITHOUT HIM,
NOT OUT ON A LIMB,
I'M ON MY OWN.
I'M ON THE TRACK
AND THERE'S NO LOOKING BACK,
I'M ON MY OWN,
ON MY OWN,
ON MY OWN.

ACT ONE

Scene 3

THE THIRD SESSION

MICHELLE. (*Doorbell.*) Coming. Mandy. You're early.
MANDY. I am?
MICHELLE. A few minutes. Come in. I was just setting up.
MANDY. Oh.
MICHELLE. Your mother called and said she won't be able to pick you up.
MANDY. Did she say it was my mother?
MICHELLE. Let me see. (*Checks pad on desk.*) Entertaining some friends tonight. Better if you didn't stay over. Take train back to school and your father will give you a call tomorrow. So I assumed . . .

MANDY. Can I use your phone?
MICHELLE. Sure. (MANDY *starts to cross to phone.*)
MANDY. Never mind. She couldn't care less, anyway.
MICHELLE. Who?
MANDY. My father's wife.
MICHELLE. She sounded very nice.
MANDY. Yeah.
MICHELLE. Parents divorced?
MANDY. No. My mother died when I was little.
MICHELLE. Oh. You don't get along with your stepmother?
MANDY. She's O.K.
MICHELLE. Your enthusiasm is overwhelming. What's the trouble there?
MANDY. There's no trouble.
MICHELLE. Really?
MANDY. Look, I don't need to be analyzed.
MICHELLE. Since you don't open up in the group, I thought you might . . .
MANDY. Neither do you.
MICHELLE. That's different.
MANDY. Why?
MICHELLE. I'm the leader. I'm the teacher.
MANDY. Why do you do these groups?
MICHELLE. I like helping people. And I like eating, paying my rent.
MANDY. Do you have a lot of lovers?
MICHELLE. So now *I'm* on the couch.
MANDY. Who with?
MICHELLE. Ha. Ha. Ha. Press conference over. (*DOORBELL.*) Coming! (*DOOORBELL rings again.* MANDY, *upon hearing "Beth", slouches in front of desk, hiding.*) Beth, how are you?
BETH. (*Slight pause.*) Is that a person-to-person question or a shrink-to-patient question?
MICHELLE. Person-to-person I guess.
BETH. (*With mock relief.*) Good. Then I'm fine, thank you, and you?
MICHELLE. Fine. I'll just be a minute. (MICHELLE *exits to other part of loft.* BETH *hangs up her coat, then stops in front of the mirror to put on a doctor's white hospital coat and stethoscope.* MANDY *pops up suddenly.*)
MANDY. Hello!
BETH. Oh. Hello.

MICHELLE. What in the world are you wearing?
BETH. I guess you forgot to do this week's assignment.
MANDY. I don't do the assignments.
BETH. "I don't do the assignments." The aspiring doctor is too busy with her school work?
MANDY. Mmm.
BETH. I bet you're a top student. (*Pause.*) Aren't you?
MANDY. Yeah.
BETH. Straight A's?
MANDY. Pretty much.
BETH. I bet you make your mother real proud of you. (*Pause.*) Well, Madame Curie? (*DOORBELL. MICHELLE enters. SHE senses the usual tension between MANDY and BETH.*)
MICHELLE. Looks like you two are having a friendly chat. (MICHELLE *opens door, several* WOMEN *enter.*)
ALICE. This you won't believe.
MICHELLE. What, that Sherry's on time?
ALICE. No, her outfit. (SHERRY *appears dressed as a pregnant housewife.*)
SHERRY. Hi you guys! (GWEN *enters, wearing what she considers to be a chic Soho artist's get-up complete with beret; she looks ridiculous.*)
GWEN. Hey, man! Far out! (*DOORBELL.* MICHELLE *answers and* EILEEN *enters, wearing a man's business suit.*)
EILEEN. Hello. I just couldn't decide what to wear.
MICHELLE. We'll start with you, Eileen.
EILEEN. Oh, all right. You know, I feel kind of dumb. I wore a tie, because I want to be a businesswoman, and I realized that's pretty sexist of me—wearing a tie—as if you had to be a man to be in business, but every time I took off the tie and looked in the mirror, I didn't look like a businesswoman.
MICHELLE. When did you decide you wanted to go into business?
EILEEN. This week.
MICHELLE. Does anyone have any comments about Eileen's conflict over the tie?
SHERRY. I think it looks better with it.
MICHELLE. Why?
SHERRY. Beats me.
MICHELLE. How many of you would take financial advice from a woman as readily as from a man? (*No one answers.*) Interesting, isn't it? How many of you have women doctors?

ALICE. I would never go to a woman doctor.
MANDY. That's ridiculous. There are a lot of brilliant women doctors.
MICHELLE. Do you go to one, Mandy?
MANDY. (*Pause.*) (*Uncomfortable.*) That's not the point.
MICHELLE. Alice?
ALICE. Yeah?
MICHELLE. Can you show us your costume?
ALICE. (*Uneasily, with coat still on.*) Not yet. I'm cold.
MICHELLE. Gwen?
GWEN. Well, last year I took a class in painting at the Westchester Community College and in the spring I took their History of Art course, and ever since then I've been a real art fan. I go to museums and I even do a bit of painting myself.
MICHELLE. Good. You should keep it up.
GWEN. Oh, I intend to.
SHERRY. Gwen, you could start your own gallery or something.
GWEN. Well, I don't know.
SHERRY. Really. Like "Gwen's Art Design Limited."
GWEN. Very limited.
MICHELLE. Don't put yourself down. Beth, what about you?
BETH. (*Snidely, to* MICHELLE.) I came as I *would* have been.
MICHELLE. (*Cooly.*) Oh, I see. Well, we'll talk about that later. Sherry? (*Taken aback,* BETH *remains standing for a moment, then sits.*)
SHERRY. Well, for the "Come as You'll Be" exercise, I came as a housewife.
GWEN. (*Appalled.*) Why?
SHERRY. 'Cause that's what I want to be.
BETH. You're planning to have that pillow out of wedlock?
SHERRY. No, I'm waiting for Mike to propose. I'm twenty-seven and I'm beginning to panic, you know?
GWEN. What's your hurry?
SHERRY. I want to have kids already.
ALICE. Why?
SHERRY. I think it would be really incredible.
ALICE. My dog had three litters and she didn't consider it incredible.
SHERRY. Yesterday my girlfriend stopped by with her baby boy and he kept wrapping his tiny hands around my two fingers

... It was the most beautiful feeling.

EILEEN. It is.

SHERRY. I really want to be a mother. And I want a house to decorate and clean.

GWEN. Sherry, after a few months you stop getting a kick out of clean linens and emptied wastebaskets.

EILEEN. No, I still get a thrill from cleaning the house.

BETH. Whatever turns you on.

GWEN. No one notices the work you do. Nothing. Zero. Like you don't exist.

EILEEN. Unless someone wants a favor done. Then, all of a sudden Mommy becomes popular.

SHERRY. But you must love children. You're having your fifth.

EILEEN. (*Mildly.*) Yes. Well . . . (*Then suddenly, overemphatically.*) Yes, of course!

GWEN. When you went to a party, people used to ask, "How many children do you have?" Now, it's "What do you *do*?" And when you say "I'm a housewife" you feel humiliated.

SHERRY. I'd feel proud.

MICHELLE. If Sherry wants to be a housewife, that's her decision.

ALICE. (*Gesturing to covered plate.*) Uh hem.

SHERRY. Oh! I almost forgot. As part of my duty as housewife-to-be, I baked us all a cake.

GWEN. Great!

EILEEN. What kind of cake is it?

SHERRY. It's carrot cake with cream cheese frosting. (SHERRY *presents the cake;* OTHERS *ad lib "It looks delicious", etc.*)

BETH. (*Reading off cake.*) Happy "Come as You'll Be" . . . from your devoted wife and mother, Sherry . . . to all of my friends in the Women's Ass Training Workshop?

SHERRY. I couldn't fit the whole word.

MICHELLE. It does look very good. Should we wait until the break?

GWEN. Nah.

ALICE. It might get stale.

MICHELLE. All right.

SHERRY. (*Slices cake, and passes it.*) Here we go.

MANDY. It smells great.

BETH. (BETH *intercepts the piece to* MANDY, *gives it to* ALICE *instead. She over-enunciates "t" of audit.*) Mandy gets to audi*t* the cake.

I CAN'T KEEP RUNNING IN PLACE

SHERRY. Michelle?
MICHELLE. Thank you. (MICHELLE *takes a piece of cake to* MANDY.)
MANDY. Alice! That's 2nds you're going on.
ALICE. Yeah. But who's counting, right?
GWEN. She's allowed. It's a party.
ALICE. Yeah, parties are the only time I'm allowed to cheat.
MICHELLE. You only cheat at parties?
ALICE. No, I cheat all the time. But parties are the only time I'm *allowed*.
MANDY. But Alice used to be thin. Alice, show them the picture of you.
ALICE. Come on, Mandy.
SHERRY. You could lose the weight. You should jog like me.
ALICE. Right. Half of me would be in the village while the other half is still on 79th Street.
GWEN. Right.
SHERRY. You could too, Gwen.
GWEN. No, I've tried.
SHERRY. I know some great health diets. There's a terrific water and lettuce diet.
ALICE. Sounds yummy.
SHERRY. Gwen, you should try it. You really could lose.
GWEN. No, I can't. I've tried, and I can't.

(*MUSIC.*)

"MORE OF ME TO LOVE"

(GWEN *and* ALICE.)
GWEN.
OH, I DID EVERY DIET, AND FAT FARM AND CLINIC,
WELL, NOW I WON'T BUY IT, 'CAUSE NOW I'M A CYNIC.
I STILL WEAR A DOUBLE DD BRA,
I DESPISE THE SIZE OF MY THIGHS,
AFTER HUFFING AND PUFFING
TWO MONTHS AT THE SPA,
THEY GAVE ME THE (*Indicates bust.*) BOOBY PRIZE.
SOMETIMES I REALLY RESENT,
ALL THE TIME AND THE MONEY I SPENT,
ON THE POTIONS AND LOTIONS,
PHYSICIANS, BEAUTICIANS,
GOD, IT'S A CRIME,

BUT I TRIED ONE LAST TIME,
AND I WENT TO THE BEST CENTRAL PARK WEST DIETICIAN.
(GWEN *nibbles unconsciously.*)
OH, I CAN'T LOSE WEIGHT,
NO, I CAN'T LOSE WEIGHT,
IT SEEMS IT'S IN MY GENES,
IT SEEMS IT'S JUST MY FATE.
   ALICE.
IF SHYLOCK WANTS ONE POUND OF FLESH,
WE'D GIVE HIM EIGHT!
   GWEN.
OH, I CAN'T LOSE WEIGHT!
NO, I CAN'T LOSE WEIGHT!

THE DOCTOR SAID TO EAT CARROTS, TOMATO, AND COTTAGE CHEESE,
DRY TOAST WITHOUT ANY JELLY,
BUT ON THE NINTH VISIT,
HE ASKED ME, "WHY IS IT,
THERE'S FLAB ON YOUR TUSH AND ON YOUR BELLY?"

I'VE BEEN SINCERE,
NO ONION DIPS,
I WORKED ON MY REAR,
I WORKED ON MY HIPS . . .
   ALICE.
YOU WORKED ON SIX BAGS OF POTATO CHIPS!
   GWEN.
NO, I CAN'T LOSE WEIGHT.
OH, I CAN'T LOSE WEIGHT.
IT'S GLANDULAR, I'M SURE,
OR ELSE IT'S JUST MY FATE.
   ALICE.
YOU'D BE THIN IF DISCIPLINE WAS SOMETHING YA ATE!
   GWEN.
OH, I CAN'T LOSE WEIGHT.
(*MUSIC vamps.*)
   ALICE. It's taken me over three years to get to where I am. Why in the world would you want to lose weight?

(*Spoken.*)
Expensive cars are big,
And classic books are thick,
Everyone loves Porky Pig,
Everyone loves Saint Nick!
(*Sexily.*)
NOW THERE'S MORE OF ME TO LOVE,
MORE OF ME TO SQUEEZE,
MORE OF ME TO KISS,
MORE OF ME TO PLEASE.

MORE OF ME TO SMOOCH,
MORE OF ME TO GRIP,
MORE TO GOOCHY-GOOCH,
MORE OF ME TO STRIP.
(*Takes off her coat and reveals a sexy torch singer outfit.*)
SOON MEN WILL THRONG TO ME,
I DON'T LOOK LIKE KING KONG, TO ME.
SOON THEY'LL ALL BE RUSHING TO MY SIDE,
PETER, JONATHAN AND JOE,
CAN'T ANYBODY SEE I'M SO MAGNIFICENT . . .
   GWEN.
INSIDE!
   ALICE.
NOW THERE'S . . .
MORE OF ME TO PINCH,
WITH MORE YOU CAN DO PLENTY,
WHAT'S AN EXTRA INCH?
   GWEN.
WHAT'S AN EXTRA TWENTY?
   ALICE.
MORE OF ME TO KNOW,
(*Indicates rear.*) MORE FROM CHEEK TO CHEEK,
GO FROM HEAD TO TOE,
   GWEN.
THAT COULD TAKE A WEEK!
   ALICE.
ONE DAY I GOT A CALL,
FROM AN ACTOR, SLIGHT AND SMALL,
AND HOW I DEARLY MOTHERED HIM,
BUT NOW HIS CALLS ARE SELDOM,

'CAUSE THE LAST TIME THAT I HELD HIM,
I NEARLY SMOTHERED HIM.
AND NOW THERE'S . . .

LESS OF HIM TO LOVE,
(*Searches for him.*)
LESS OF HIM TO GRIP,
LESS OF HIM TO SQUEEZE,
LESS OF HIM TO WHIP!
(*Makes a whipping motion.*)

AND SO MUCH
MORE OF ME TO NESTLE,
 GWEN.
MORE FROM HIP TO HIP,
 ALICE.
MORE OF ME TO WRESTLE,
 GWEN.
MORE OF ME TO . . .
 ALICE. (*Sexily.*) Whatever!
 GWEN.
OH, I'VE SHED THE SKIN OF THE SKINNY ME.
 ALICE.
GOOD RIDDANCE TO THE MINI ME.
 GWEN AND ALICE.
THAT CELERY STICK AND WHEAT THINNY ME,
 ALICE.
I'LL BE A PUDGY ME!
 GWEN.
A CHOCOLATE FUDGY ME!
 ALICE AND GWEN.
AND THERE WILL ALWAYS,
THERE WILL ALWAYS,
THERE WILL ALWAYS BE . . .
 GWEN.
MORE OF ME TO
 ALICE.
AH!
 GWEN.
MORE OF ME TO
 ALICE.
OOO!

GWEN.
MORE OF ME TO
ALICE.
MMMMMM!
ALICE AND GWEN.
MORE OF ME TO LOVE!

MANDY. I still don't get the boa bit.
ALICE. (*With Garbo accent.*) Vat? Don't you like eet?
MANDY. Are you trying to be symbolic or something?
ALICE. Or something. Actress. Skeeny actress.
MICHELLE. I thought you said you were already an actress?
ALICE. I vas. But not right now.
MICHELLE. Why not?
ALICE. Pass.
MANDY. What?
ALICE. Pass. (*Very melodramatic.*) I vant to be alone.
MANDY. But why'd you go all out and dress up if you don't want to talk about it?
BETH. (*To* MICHELLE, *while taking off her stethoscope and Dr. coat.*) Because then she felt like it and now she doesn't.
ALICE. Right.
GWEN. (*Talks to relieve tension in room.*) I just realized, I did cheat once this month. Jerome took the kids on a ski trip and there was just me and the refrigerator.
SHERRY. Oh, I know. When I'm alone, I really let myself go.
ALICE. What do you pig out on? Celery juice?
GWEN. I feel sorry for women who live alone.
EILEEN. Sometimes I envy them.
SHERRY. I really can't live by myself without a man. It gives me the jitters. I'm so much happier now that I have someone.
ALICE. I have a lot more spare time because I *don't* have someone. I spend most of my spare time convincing myself that I'm lucky to have spare time.
SHERRY. I really want to share my life with someone I love.
BETH. Oh, God.
SHERRY. You seem to like living alone, Michelle.
MICHELLE. I do.
SHERRY. Where are your children?
MICHELLE. In Boston.
SHERRY. With your husband?
MICHELLE. (*Nods.*) Mm hm.

EILEEN. Are you seeing anyone else?
MICHELLE. Paul Newman.
SHERRY. Don't the courts usually give the children to . . .
MICHELLE. (*Getting up, uncomfortable.*) We haven't been to court. We're just separated. Look, we're not here to discuss me.
BETH. So you're all alone.
MICHELLE. Not "all alone". Alone. Now, are you ready yet, Beth?
BETH. For what?
MICHELLE. To tell us something about yourself?
BETH. Pick a topic, any topic. Except age.
MICHELLE. How about living alone?
BETH. (*Pauses, smiles glibly.*) Now, how did you know I live alone?
MICHELLE. Intuition.
BETH. Ladies and Gentlemen, Beth Gilbert, known for her talent in living alone.

"I LIVE ALONE"

BETH. (*Addresses the group.*)
AT NIGHT, IN BED,
I LIE AWAKE TO DREAM,
I DREAM OF A MAN BESIDE ME:
A MAN WHO MIGHT WELCOME MY AFFECTION,
A MAN WHO MIGHT FEEL MY HAND UPON HIS SHOULDER.

THE RHYTHM OF HIS BREATH
ACCOMPANIES MY OWN
AS WE IMPROVISE A SONG.
WE TOSS THE MELODY BACK AND FORTH,
MAKING UP THE WORDS AS WE GO ALONG.

I LIVE ALONE
IN A LARGE HOUSE
WITH PLENTY OF ROOM—FOR LONELINESS.
AN EMPTY SPACE
FILLED WITH SILENCE AND ANTIQUE FURNITURE,
I AM ALONE . . .

(*Becoming introspective.*)

I CAN'T KEEP RUNNING IN PLACE

SOMETIMES IT SEEMS
THAT I KNOW HIM,
THIS LOVING MAN I DREAM ABOUT,
WE SING OUT LOUD,
AND FOR A MOMENT I'M ABLE TO FORGET
I AM ALONE . . .

(*Deeper in thought.*)

BUT I LISTEN TO THE SONG
AND IT ALWAYS SEEMS
THAT MY VOICE IS STRONG
ONLY IN MY DREAMS,
FOR I'VE GROWN HOARSE FROM MOUTHING WORDS
THAT NO ONE LISTENS TO.
MOCKED BY SILENCE,
I PERFORM MY LIFE BEFORE AN EMPTY HOUSE.

I'M ACCUSTOMED NOW TO LONELY NIGHTS,
NIGHTS WITHOUT A LOVING MAN,
I LET FLIGHTS OF MIND TAKE ME WHERE THEY CAN,
I INDULGE IN DREAMS AND FANTASY
IN ORDER TO FORGET . . .

(*Suddenly, aware again of the group.*)

I LIVE ALONE
IN A LARGE HOUSE
WITH PLENTY OF ROOM—FOR LONELINESS.
AN EMPTY SPACE
FILLED WITH SILENCE AND ANTIQUE FURNITURE,
I AM ALONE . . .

(*To* MICHELLE.)

AND MARRIED.

   MICHELLE. How long have you been married?
   BETH. Almost twenty-three years.
   MICHELLE. Do you have children?
   BETH. One. One child, one dog, one husband.
   MICHELLE. Is that in order of preference?
   BETH. (*Smiles.*) Let's just say I have a husband in name only.

At dinner, Carl (my husband) studies the gum X-rays for the next day's operations. He's a periodontist. He gets up before me, goes to sleep before me. Nine-thirty.

SHERRY. Really?

BETH. Well, that is not entirely fair of me. On big occasions Carl has been known to make it until ten-thirty. And Saturday nights, it's more like eleven. Saturday nights we go out to dinner with a colleague of Carl's and his colleague's wife, which means I have the distinct privilege of knowing every oral surgeon at Columbia Presbyterian and of knowing not a negligible amount about the operative techniques which Carl et al. do not hesitate to discuss at the dinner table. And it's not that I mind learning about nerve ending spasms and receding bicuspids. Oh, no. Don't get me wrong. I mean, on Saturday night it's nice to learn something about your husband's technique.

MANDY. But why were *you* wearing the doctor get up?

BETH. (*Proudly, directed at* MANDY.) Because, I would have been a doctor. (*Now addressing the group.*) I was in my second year at Med School when I married Carl, who felt it would be wiser for me to drop out of school, temporarily, in order to support him while he continued, and then once he was somewhat established, why, he would send me. But . . . by the time Carl finished his residency, I was pregnant, so I learned to confine my medical talent to administering Bayer Aspirin when my kid was home sick. Which she's not anymore. She's at school now. Which tends to make dinner conversations between Carl and myself a little dull since Carl does not talk. Not really, anyway. So there we sit, night after night at the dinner table, Carl studying his gums, me getting together my ideas to write the great American novel.

GWEN. Oh, you write!

BETH. Yes, I write.

MICHELLE. Do you publish?

BETH. I write.

EILEEN. Things were better when your daughter was still at home?

BETH. Well, at least I had Amy to keep me busy. Now that she's at med school — Johns Hopkins — terribly brilliant. Takes after her mother. I'm very proud of her. She knows what she wants and she doesn't let a lot of people clutter up her life. Going straight to the top, that girl. She is going to be a well known surgeon and follow in her father's footsteps. Not gums, though. I made her swear it would not be gums.

EILEEN. It must be wonderful having a daughter.
BETH. (*Evasive.*) It is. (*Pause.*) Beth Gilbert also likes tennis, writing poetry, collecting antiques and sewing buttons. A grrrrrrrrreat gal . . . Lucky to have her here with us tonight . . . heeere she is . . . Beth Gilbert. One of the most frustrated women in the New York metropolitan area.
SHERRY. If you're so unhappy, why are you still married?
BETH. Habit. (BETH *waits for* MICHELLE'S *response, but* MICHELLE *turns her attention to* ALICE.)
MICHELLE. Alice, can you tell us something about your costume?
ALICE. Sure. It's hand washable.
MICHELLE. Come on. What are you going to be?
ALICE. Well, I'm not going to be married, that's for sure.
SHERRY. Is it that rotten?
MICHELLE. What?
SHERRY. Marriage. The way you all talk you'd think . . .
BETH. No, not rotten. You can only say something is rotten if it was good at one time.
GWEN. Marriage is a sort of investment. You get out of it what you put into it.
BETH. That's what they said in '29 before the crash.
MANDY. I'd never let that happen. I'd never marry anyone if I wasn't sure it was going to work.
BETH. It happens. One day you wake up and you say to yourself, "My God, where am I? (*Jolting, as if seeing a stranger next to her in bed.*) Who is the man lying in bed next to me?"
ALICE. (*Casually.*) That's what I'm always saying after a one-night stand.
BETH. Just think! I've been having a one-night stand for twenty-three years.
SHERRY. (*Taking out the pillow from her costume.*) I give up. You guys are too gloomy for me.
MICHELLE. Alice, why are you so skeptical?
ALICE. Guys are always screwing me over.
MICHELLE. How so?
ALICE. By being dishonest.
MICHELLE. And you've never been guilty of that?
ALICE. No.
MICHELLE. What about when a man calls who you're not interested in dating?
ALICE. That would never happen.
MICHELLE. Come on, Alice.

ALICE. I'm very polite and whenever he calls I tell him I happen to be busy . . . till he gets the hint.

MICHELLE. Alice, that's a cop out. You think you're being considerate but you're really being evasive, and you're very good at that.

ALICE. So the next time he calls, I'll be more direct. "Warren, you have crust in your eyes and you're dull and No Thanks."

MICHELLE. Have you ever had a long term relationship?

ALICE. Sure. (*With confidence.*) Two weeks.

MANDY. Sounds like you *have* been screwed over.

ALICE. Actually, when I think back on the relationships I've had, (*MUSIC begins.*) I can't think of one man that I couldn't count on.

(ALICE *and* COMPANY.)

"I CAN COUNT ON YOU"

WHEN I NEED YOU,

I CAN COUNT ON YOU . . .
NOT TO BE THERE,
I CAN TRUST IN YOU . . .
NOT TO CARE,
I CAN DEPEND ON YOU . . .
LIKE I CAN FLOAT IN AIR.

(*Takes out feather boa from bag, uses during song.*)

WHEN I NEED YOU,

I CAN COUNT ON YOU . . .
ALWAYS TO LEAVE ME,
I CAN TRUST IN YOU . . .
TO DECEIVE ME,
I CAN DEPEND ON YOU . . .
LIKE I CAN FLOAT IN AIR.

WHEN I NEED,
SOMEONE TO HOLD ME,
NOT JUST TO SCOLD ME,
YOU'RE NOT THERE!
(WHERE ARE YOU?)

I CAN'T KEEP RUNNING IN PLACE 43

WHEN I NEED,
SOMEONE TO GUIDE ME,
NOT TO DERIDE ME,
YOU DON'T CARE!
(WHERE ARE YOU?)

WHEN I NEED YOU,

I CAN COUNT ON YOU . . .
NOT TO BE THERE,
I CAN TRUST IN YOU . . .
NOT TO CARE,
I CAN DEPEND ON YOU . . .
LIKE I CAN FLOAT IN AIR.

(*Instrumental begins. MUSIC stops abruptly. The following sketches should have a vaudeville quality.*)

ALICE. (*Continued.*) But, Peter, it's my birthday. Why are you taking *her* out to dinner?
SHERRY. (*Peter.*) (*Thinks, then.*) To celebrate your birthday? (*Short phrase of MUSIC.*)
ALICE. Donald! I have so much to tell you!
BETH. (*Donald.*) (*Thinks, then.*) Great! Send me a cassette! (*Short phrase of MUSIC.*)
ALICE. (*Upset.*) Jonathan! I'm pregnant!
EILEEN. (*Jonathan.*) Congratulations!
BETH.
SORRY!
GWEN.
BUSY!
SHERRY.
TIRED!
EILEEN.
LATER!
BETH, GWEN, SHERRY, EILEEN.
SORRY! BUSY! TIRED! LATER!
SORRY! BUSY! TIRED! LATER! OO WAH!
SORRY! BUSY! TIRED! LATER! OO WAH!

(*DANCE/Scene.*)
(*The choreography should have a comic tone. The dance shows*

*several "*MEN*" rejecting* ALICE. BETH, EILEEN, GWEN, *and* SHERRY *will play several roles, male and female.* MICHELLE *and* MANDY *observe, amused.*

Accompanied by a provocative drum solo, ALICE *crosses downstage to make herself up and prepare for her date. She pretends to apply lipstick, line her eyebrows, and lift each breast into her "dress." Her primping should take the form of a comic, stylized, choreographic bit, which will be repeated several times during the scene, always accompanied by the drum solo.* ALICE *and* MAN 1 *begin to dance, when* WOMAN 1 *appears.* MAN 1 *tosses* ALICE *aside, and dances with* WOMAN 1.

MAN 2 *crosses to* ALICE. *Eager for a second chance,* ALICE *prepares for her new date and joins her partner.* THEY *dance a step or two, but when* MAN 2 *catches the eye of* WOMAN 2, *he twirls* ALICE *in a turn and purposely lets go of her hand:* ALICE *goes flying and* MAN 2 *pursues* WOMAN 2.

ALICE, *distraught, runs upstage and catches the eye of* MAN 3. *In a last chance panic,* ALICE *primps herself one last time.*

SHE *dances joyfully with* MAN 3, *thinking she has found a lasting companion. In their final dip, however,* MAN 3 *catches a glimpse of* WOMAN 3; HE *lets* ALICE *fall on her rear, and pursues his new interest.)*

   BETH.
WHEN I NEED
SOMEONE TO BE WITH,
   EILEEN.
SOMEONE TO AGREE WITH ME,
   BOTH.
WHERE ARE YOU?
   GWEN.
WHEN I NEED
SOMEONE TO CRY WITH,
   SHERRY.
NOT JUST TO LIE WITH,
YOU'RE NOT FREE.
   BOTH.
WHERE ARE YOU?

(MANDY *and* MICHELLE *join, each involved in her own private thoughts.)*

I CAN'T KEEP RUNNING IN PLACE

ALL.
WHEN I NEED YOU,
I CAN COUNT ON YOU . . .
NOT TO BE THERE.
I CAN TRUST IN YOU . . .
NOT TO CARE.
I CAN DEPEND ON YOU . . .
LIKE I CAN FLOAT IN AIR.

(ALICE *joins the* WOMEN *with a high scat.*)

ALICE.
AH . . . WHERE ARE YOU?
WHERE ARE YOU? OO . . .
ALL.
WHEN I NEED YOU,
I CAN COUNT ON YOU,
ALWAYS TO LEAVE ME,
I CAN TRUST IN YOU,
TO DECEIVE ME,
ALICE. (*Continued.*)
I CAN DEPEND ON YOU,
LIKE I CAN FLOAT
IN . . .
ALL.
AIR!

BLACKOUT.

ACT TWO

Scene 1

THE FIFTH SESSION

*Role-playing lights up on a "*Man*" and* Woman *in "bed," facing audience, (using cushions or 4 chairs, arranged as a bed). The following scene is a role-playing exercise between* Sherry, *who is playing herself, and* Alice, *who is portraying* Mike, Sherry's *lover.)*

Alice. (*Mike.*) Wow!
Sherry. Hm?
Alice. (*Mike.*) I said WOW! Incredible.
Sherry. Oh . . . yeah, why, sure.
Alice. (*Mike.*) Mmmhm. Wow.
Sherry. Yeah. (*Pause.*) Mike?
Alice. (*Mike.*) Yes, Tigress?
Sherry. (*Taking a deep breath, mustering courage.*) I was not really into it sexually, Mike. All the feeling is there, but I don't seem to be able to . . . (She *interrupts herself and addresses* Michelle.) I could *never* say that.
Michelle. Go ahead. Try. What do you have to lose?
Sherry. Yeah, all right. (*To* Alice/Mike.) Mike?
Alice. (*Mike.*) Would you scratch my back, honey?
Sherry. Do you hear what I'm trying to say, Mike?
Alice. (*Mike.*) Yes, honey. I think I understand. But I'm pretty surprised. I mean, no woman has been that open with me in bed, ya know?
Sherry. I'm sorry if . . .
Alice. (*Mike.*) Don't be sorry. I understand.
Sherry. You do? Great.
Alice. (*Mike.*) Don't stop scratching.
Sherry. Because sex is supposed to be good for both people involved . . . and we've been sleeping together for three months now and well . . . nothing has ever happened. I mean, I've enjoyed sleeping with you, it's just that . . .
Alice. (*Mike.*) (*Getting an idea.*) Don't feel awkward about it, honey. I understand there's a problem.
Sherry. Yeah. And it has nothing to do with my feelings for you.

ALICE. (*Mike.*) I know that. Really, honey, I had no idea, but why didn't you tell me before?

SHERRY. I thought you would get angry, or defensive.

ALICE. (*Mike.*) You thought *I* would get defensive because *you're* frigid? (*There is a burst of laughter from the* WOMEN.)

SHERRY. (*Shocked.*) What?

MICHELLE. That's what happens when you beat around the bush.

MANDY. Tell him he's an egocentric ass!

MICHELLE. Why? It's not really his fault.

ALICE. Sherry didn't say what she wanted to say. She wasn't specific about the problem. She just hinted, so I threw her a curve.

EILEEN. Well, who wants to get clinical? I'm opposed to those manuals where you do it by numbers.

MICHELLE. No, Alice is right. If you are going to be assertive you've got to be clear and to the point, right? So why should sex be any different?

SHERRY. He really isn't a bad lover.

MICHELLE. Then maybe you should start by telling him that.

SHERRY. I just know that there are certain things that . . . well, if he did them, I know I could have, well . . .

MICHELLE. Have an orgasm?

SHERRY. Well, yes.

MICHELLE. O.K. So, say it. (MICHELLE *motions toward the "bed."* SHERRY *starts but* ALICE/Mike *gives her a "ready and willing" look, and* SHERRY *retreats to her seat.*)

SHERRY. Well, actually, when you think about it, what difference does it make if I gave Mike the impression that I was frigid instead of making him feel that he hadn't been doing all the right things for me? I mean, either way, he'd work harder at it.

MICHELLE. But, Sherry, he won't know what to work harder at! And even on principle, you'd prefer to have Mike think you're frigid?

SHERRY. No. It's just that I don't want to hurt his feelings. I really like him. And I don't want to lose him.

MICHELLE. Why should you sleep with Mike, night after night, always frustrated, silently thinking, "If he'd only do this, if only, if only, then I might . . ."

BETH. Jesus, if you're going to do that, you might as well be married!

ALICE. I just wish all women were biologically unable to have orgasms.

SHERRY. Are you crazy?

ALICE. No. Then I wouldn't feel so pressured. The minute I'm in bed with someone it's off to the races and I start concentrating on having an orgasm—as quickly as is humanly possible—I mean I feel obligated to have one.

SHERRY. You mean, it's like it's for his sake so *he* doesn't feel bad.

ALICE. No. I just feel as if I'm competing with all the other women he's ever been with. If he does ask, and I didn't have one, I feel inadequate.

MICHELLE. How do you think *he* feels when he asks and you say "No, I didn't."

ALICE. I never thought about it.

MICHELLE. You should. He might be feeling that *he's* inadequate.

ALICE. All I know is I resent it when they ask.

SHERRY. I resent it when they *don't* ask.

ALICE. They ask to satisfy their own egos.

SHERRY. They don't ask because they don't care.

MICHELLE. Don't you think you're both being unfair? You're putting *your* resentment and hung-up energy on *him*.

SHERRY. There *are* some men that really don't care.

MICHELLE. Yes, but most men are just as uptight about discussing it as we are.

ALICE. But his asking is embarrassing. I just wish he'd leave me alone.

MICHELLE. They why are you in bed with him? (ALICE *starts to shrug, then breaks into a smile, acknowledging* MICHELLE's *point.*) Anyway, a man shouldn't have to ask "did you?" If you're really communicating when you should be, then it's more likely that you will have the orgasm and he won't have to ask.

ALICE. Sometimes the whole thing gets me so anxious I just wish it would just be over with so I could go home and recover.

BETH. You make it sould like root canal.

SHERRY. (*To* MICHELLE *privately.*) Michelle, I know you're right. I mean I love every minute I spend with Mike out of bed and I want to love the time we spend together in bed. I'd love to have . . . I mean, I'd love to have a fulfilling . . .

MICHELLE. You mean you want to have an orgasm. Who doesn't? Look, the more you assert yourself in anxiety-

I CAN'T KEEP RUNNING IN PLACE 49

producing situations, the more comfortable you will be the next time you encounter the situation. Soooooo . . . repeat after me. Orgasm. (*The* WOMEN *laugh.*) I'm serious. Orgasm.

WOMEN. (*Softly and abashedly, or making fun of the exercise.*) Orgasm.

MICHELLE. Orgasm.

WOMEN. (*Still softly.*) Orgasm.

MICHELLE. (*Like a cheer.*) Louder!

WOMEN. (*A little louder.*) Orgasm.

MICHELLE. Louder!

WOMEN. Orgasm.

MICHELLE. Now, repeat after me. "I'd like to talk to you."

WOMEN. (*Loudly.*) I'd like to talk to you . . .

MICHELLE. About the fact . . .

WOMEN. (*Loudly.*) About the fact . . .

MICHELLE. That when we make love . . .

WOMEN. (*Loudly.*) That when we make love . . .

MICHELLE. Good. I never have . . .

WOMEN. (*Loudly.*) I never have . . .

MICHELLE. . . . an orgasm.

WOMEN. (*Softly.*) . . . an orgasm.

MICHELLE. A WHAT?

WOMEN. An orgasm.

MICHELLE. (*Speaking quietly and with great energy, pointing to every other woman.*) Now the whole thing. Each of you tell your man next to you. Go!

GWEN, SHERRY, EILEEN. (*Softly, and very quickly.*) I'd like to talk to you about the fact that when we make love I never have an orgasm.

MICHELLE. Now switch.

ALICE, MANDY, BETH. (*Softly and very quickly.*) I'd like to talk to you about the fact that when we make love I never have an orgasm. (*The following should continue to crescendo in volume and excitement.*)

MICHELLE. Now, give me an O!

WOMEN. O.

MICHELLE. Give me an R!

WOMEN. R.

MICHELLE. Give me a G!

WOMEN. Geeeeeeee.

MICHELLE. Give me an A!

WOMEN. A.

MICHELLE. Give me an S!
WOMEN. S.
MICHELLE. And an M!
WOMEN. M.
MICHELLE. Give me an ORGASM!
WOMEN. (*Enjoying the absurdity and the release.*) ORGASM!
MICHELLE. What?
WOMEN. (*Screaming it.*) ORGASM! (*The* WOMEN *laugh and react for several seconds.*)
SHERRY. Ya know, the next time I'm with Mike, I'm really going to try to talk about it. I'll just have to remember rehearsing it here.
BETH. Yeah, I can just picture it. You're in the middle of an intimate love scene and you hop out of bed to get your pompoms and start screaming, "Yea Orgasm!"
SHERRY. Very funny, Beth.
MICHELLE. If I had a nickel for every woman who had trouble talking about orgasm . . .
BETH. Better than that, if you had an *orgasm* for every woman who couldn't talk about orgasm! Anyway, I thought you young people didn't have any trouble saying words like screw, ball, penis . . .
SHERRY. (*Boldly.*) Penis, penis, penis, penis, penis. I do that one really well. You see, I was in this sensitivity workshop where all the women in the group had to pretend they had penises.
BETH. Peni.
MANDY. (*Snidely, to* BETH.) Actually, the plural is either penes, (P.E.N.E.S.) or plain old penises. (P.E.N.I.S.E.S.) From the Latin word, tail.
BETH. Really?
MANDY. Uh huh.
BETH. (*With mock admiration.*) One never stops learning.
MICHELLE. Sherry, who made you do that exercise?
SHERRY. The psychiatrist who led the workshop.
MICHELLE. What's his name?
SHERRY. I don't remember her name.
MICHELLE. It was a woman?
SHERRY. Yeah. She said that all women are victims of Penis Envy and it would help our condition to make believe.
MICHELLE. Incredible. What else did she say?
SHERRY. She said that the reason young girls like horseback riding is because they can imagine that the horsey between their legs is a huge penis.

EILEEN. (*Covers mouth with hand, thinking she is about to get sick.*) That's disgusting!

SHERRY. It sounded silly to me, but I kinda lost interest in riding.

BETH. That theory does not do a hell of a lot for the image of little Liz Taylor and her National Velvet.

MICHELLE. I'm afraid I disagree with your Ms. Sensitivity psychiatrist.

GWEN. I wouldn't want one of those things.

BETH. No one's offering you one.

MICHELLE. Listen, are our bodies incomplete?

ALL. No!

MICHELLE. Come on, everybody. We have a score to settle with Mr. Freud.

"PENIS ENVY" (*An Operatic Aria.*)

(*On each ascending "AH," MICHELLE raises her arm a bit higher, in the traditional operatic style. She gracefully brings her arm back to her body before outstretching it again on the next "AH." By the third "AH," her arm is shoulder level, at a 90 degree angle to her body. On the final "AH," SHE thrusts her arm straight over her head, so that her arm is in line with her body. This will have a comic effect, since the final "AH" is an unexpected low note.*)

MICHELLE.
AH, AH, AH, AH!

PENIS ENVY, PENIS ENVY,
DID VENUS ENVY ADONIS' CROTCH?
PSYCHIATRISTS TELL US
FREUD WAS RIGHT WHEN HE STATED,
WOMEN ARE JEALOUS,
AND MIGHT FEEL CASTRATED.
THERE IS NO DOUBT ABOUT IT,
  SHERRY.
AH, AH, AH, AH!
  MICHELLE.
THOUGH WE DRUDGE ON WITHOUT IT,
  EILEEN.
AH, AH, AH, AH!

MICHELLE.
WE ARE MISSING THAT ONE SPECIAL THING
MEN HAVE HAD SINCE CREATION,
WHAT WE'VE GOT IS . . .
SHERRY.
A FAKE!
EILEEN.
A MISTAKE!
ALICE.
AN IMITATION!
EILEEN. (*Crosses to* ALICE.)
AH, AH, AH! AH, AH, AH, AH, AH, AH, AH, AH, AH!
ALICE.
AH!

(ALICE *gets* GWEN *and* EILEEN *to mime the following* ADAM *and* EVE *story as she narrates.*)

ALICE. (*Continued.*)
WE KNOW ADAM GAVE UP ONE RIB TO MAKE EVE,
TO THANK HIM THAT NIGHT,
SHE BEGAN TO EXCITE HIM.
BUT WHEN EVE CAUGHT SIGHT
OF WHAT HE KEPT FOR HIMSELF . . .
(EVE *glances at* ADAM'S *"fig-leaf area."*)
AH! SHE ATE THE APPLE TO SPITE HIM!
BECAUSE EVE HAD . . .
ALL EXCEPT MANDY.
PENIS ENVY, PENIS ENVY,
JUST *BETWEEN* US, SOME *MEN* WE KNOW
DON'T HAVE A LOT,
BUT WE STILL HAVE
PENIS ENVY, PENIS ENVY.
FOR WHATEVER THEY HAVE,
IT'S MORE THAN WE GOT!
SHERRY, MICHELLE, BETH.
IT'S WHY WOMEN FROWN,
ALICE, GWEN, EILEEN
IT'S THE REASON MEN GRIN,
ALL EXCEPT MANDY.
IT'S WHY LASSIE'S NEUROTIC,
BUT NOT RIN-TIN-TIN!

(*The Strauss-like PENIS ENVY WALTZ begins. The* WOMEN *clown around and begin to waltz, or simply stand about as if they are at a grand ball.*)

ALICE. (*As an aristocratic gentleman, affected accent.*) (*Spoken, over MUSIC.*) 'Tis a pity Marie could not make it here this evening, is it not?

SHERRY. (*As the aristocratic lady, equally affected.*) Yes, 'tis indeed a pity.

ALICE. It seems she is suffering from a dreadful case of Penis Envy.

SHERRY. Yes, they say it has grown to epidemic proportions. (SHERRY *suddenly becomes a little girl. SHE sits on the floor and pretends to make mudpies.*)

SHERRY.
PENIS ENVY, PENIS ENVY,
MOMMY AND DADDY KEEP ASKING ME WHY . . .
PENIS ENVY, PENIS ENVY,
THE MUD PIES I MAKE ARE ALL SIX INCHES HIGH!

(GWEN *steps forward as another "little girl."*)

GWEN.
I'VE BEEN A GOOD GIRL ALL DECEMBER,
I SWEAR IT, ST. NICK,
SO FOR CHRISTMAS, PRETTY PLEASE REMEMBER,
I DON'T WANT A DOLLY,
WHAT I'D LIKE IS A . . .
ALL EXCEPT MANDY.
FA LA LA LA LA, LA, LA, LA, LA!

(GWEN *has been interrupted by the* WOMEN, *who finish her sentence by singing the last musical phrase of "Deck the Halls with Boughs of Holly" ending in the musical style of a dramatic choral work.*)

ALL EXCEPT MANDY. (*Continued.*)
PENIS ENVY!
MICHELLE.
AH, AH, AH, AH, AH, AH!
ALL EXCEPT MANDY.
PENIS ENVY!

SHERRY.
AH, AH, AH, AH, AH, AH!
ALICE.
AH . . .

(ALICE *begins her note from a bent knee position and slowly straightens up. She stretches her arms way above her head, hands locked, emerging as a penis.*)

GWEN. (*Spoken.*) I wonder if men ever have Vagina Jealousy?
ALICE.
AH . . .
ALL EXCEPT MANDY. (*Bowing down and worshipping* ALICE.)
PENIS ENVY! AH, AH, AH, AH, AH, AH, AH, AH, AH, AH, AH, AH, AH, (*Spoken, meaning "so what!"*) Ah, nuts!

(*After the song, the* WOMEN *remain lively, laughing on their way back to their seats. Suddenly they grow silent, for* EILEEN *has removed her scarf.* SHE *has cut her hair and looks radically different. Her former style was traditionally feminine, now it is an egg-beater-shag.*)

EILEEN. He didn't say anything. Even if it's "I hate it," I just wish he'd say *something*.
MICHELLE. Why'd you cut it?
EILEEN. I wanted short hair. I've always had long hair that everyone admired. John in particular. It was my greatest accomplishment.
ALICE. (*Positively.*) I think that took a lot of guts.
SHERRY. Yeah, 'cause it sure looked a lot better before . . . (*Realizes.*) I mean . . . I can see why your *husband* would think so . . . He'd want that girly-type hair . . . how dumb.
MICHELLE. You didn't do it to antagonize him?
EILEEN. No. I guess I wanted to see if he'd appreciate me without my hair.
GWEN. And now you feel guilty.
EILEEN. Yeah. I do.
MANDY. He doesn't own your body, or your hair, for God's sake.
EILEEN. I know.
MANDY. I can't believe after all this time you can't confront him with that.

I CAN'T KEEP RUNNING IN PLACE

BETH. Obviously he doesn't like it.
MANDY. That's not the point. (MANDY *crosses angrily away from* BETH.)
SHERRY. You look pretty.
EILEEN. I cut it so people wouldn't keep saying that and now that's all I want to hear. Am I crazy, or what?
MANDY. You were feeling good, and you wanted to test your independence, so you were very brave.
EILEEN. I don't know.
MANDY. Sure. And now that he's ignoring you, you're back to being a coward.
SHERRY. Mandy.
MANDY. You're a little girl who needs Daddy's approval.
SHERRY. Mandy.
MANDY. Now he's got you just where he wants you. (*Silence.*) Don't you see? You're inviting him to give you a guilt trip.
MICHELLE. Mandy's onto something.
BETH. Well, well. Aren't *we* clever. Stupid pest. (MANDY *crosses farther away from* BETH *and group.*)
EILEEN. Thank you, Mandy.
GWEN. (*To relieve tension.*) Uh . . . Michelle, I've got something I'd like to roleplay if that's all right.
MICHELLE. I'm not sure Eileen is finished . . .
EILEEN. No, no. That's fine. Please go ahead, Gwen.
MICHELLE. Well . . . (*Not anxious to move on yet.*) Well, okay, what?
GWEN. Well, I had a date with a girlfriend at the Modern—there's that new sculpture exhibit that opened last Monday, and Helaine, my friend, was forty-seven minutes late—she's always late, and this time, I had really had it. So . . .
SHERRY. So you didn't tell her you were angry and instead you were a creep to her the whole afternoon.
GWEN. How'd you guess?
SHERRY. 'Cause I'm always late and people are always being creepy to me.
GWEN. I wasn't mean, I just—I tried to make her feel dumb.
BETH. Oh, well *that's* nice.
MICHELLE. Sherry, since you're always late, you play the friend and Gwen . . . do pretty much what you did then. (SHERRY *and* GWEN *confer.*)
ALICE. (*Getting an idea.*) Since everyone is being typecast, *I'll* play a masterpiece. Come on, we're going to the museum, Beth. You too, Michelle. (MICHELLE *politely refuses.* ALICE *succeeds,*

however, in getting BETH *up from her seat.* ALICE *and* BETH *confer for a moment and strike an absurd pose resembling a famous classical work of art.*)

EILEEN. You clowns!

ALICE. (*Moving only her lips.*) That's no way to speak to a work of art. Come on, Eileen. We need you. (*The* WOMEN *form a new entangled creation, resembling an absurd modern sculpture. Each new sculpture* THEY *create will be a concoction of frozen bizarre facial expressions and body configurations. Each time a new sculpture is created, they strike the new pose sharply, and freeze.*)

GWEN. Here goes. (SHERRY *takes a few steps away from the playing area and runs in place.* SHE *arrives at the "museum" out of breath.*)

SHERRY. (*Helaine.*) Gwen! Hello! Hello! You look wonderful. I can't tell you how much I appreciate your going to museums with me. I know so little about art. (THEY *observe the first modern sculpture.*)

GWEN. Doesn't that remind you very much of Boccioni's earlier works? (*The* WOMEN *immediately form a new sculpture.*)

SHERRY. (*Helaine.*) Gee, I'm afraid I'm not familiar with . . .

GWEN. (*Coolly.*) Oh, that's right.

SHERRY. (*Helaine.*) Who's Boccioni?

GWEN. My! The original sketch for Oldenberg's "Woman Entwined in Giant Electric Cord." (*Another new sculpture is quickly formed and frozen.* THEY *are enjoying themselves.*)

SHERRY. (*Helaine.*) Where does Oldenberg fit into the history of . . .

GWEN. And his 1967 "Self-projection into Women Figure to Convey Gearshift Object . . . (*The* WOMEN *are perplexed and this time,* THEY *hesitate as to the shape of the new sculpture.*) With Medusa Ornaments."

(*On "Medusa Ornaments,"* ALICE *tries to make her face look Medusa-esque and* BETH *lifts* ALICE's *hair straight out to the sides of her head.* EILEEN's *expression is equally comical.* SHERRY *takes one look at the new creation and bursts out laughing.* EILEEN, BETH, *and* ALICE *begin laughing, too, and the sculpture collapses.*)

GWEN. (*Continued.*) So much for that.

MICHELLE. Wait, wait. Gwen, before you sit down, be assertive and tell Helaine how you feel.

GWEN. (*Pauses to think, then suddenly starts screaming at* SHERRY, *chasing after her.*) Dammit, Helaine. The next time you're late, you can just . . .

MICHELLE. Whoa! (*The* WOMEN *laugh, and then, so does* GWEN.) I said assertive, not aggressive. Try again.

GWEN. My darling, dearest friend . . .

MICHELLE. Come on, for real this time.

GWEN. (*Obviously forcing herself to be nice.*) Helaine, I don't know if you're aware of this, but whenever we have a date, you're late, and it makes me get tense and angry. You're a good friend and I really don't want to be annoyed with you. So if it's not asking too much . . .

MICHELLE. Uh—no sarcasm.

GWEN. So please be on time from now on.

MICHELLE. Fine, have a seat.

SHERRY. That was really neat. Ya know, the last time I worked on being late was in my transactional analysis group.

ALICE. You did transactional analysis?

SHERRY. Uh huh.

MICHELLE. How many groups have you been in?

SHERRY. Oh lots. I mean I try everything I can. I mean, like each group swears it has the answer, and I want to know what it is.

(*MUSIC.*)

"GET THE ANSWER NOW!"

(*Spoken.*)
I string beads for Hare Krishna
I do Est, I do Tai Chi,

I DO ARICA, I DO JEHOVAH'S WITNESSES,
AND GESTALT THERAPY,
I DO EVERY GROUP IN THE BOOK,
ALTHOUGH THERE'S NOTHING WRONG WITH ME.

IT'S A WAY TO MEET A HONEY,
IT'S A WAY TO PASS THE TIME,
SO IT WAS WORTH THE MONEY THAT I SPENT,
BUT I JUST HAD A RUDE AWAKENING,
YOU MIGHT CALL IT A RAW SHOCK,
AFTER DOING NINETEEN GROUPS,
I AM INWARDLY CONTENT,

YES, MY PSYCHE FEELS DIVINE,
BUT I CANNOT PAY MY RENT.

BECAUSE . . .(*Proudly.*)

I DO HYPNOSIS,
FIFTY BUCKS A NEUROSIS,
I DO YOGA, JUDO, BIORHYTHMS, NUMEROLOGY,
TRANSACTIONAL ANALYSIS, BEHAVIORAL PSYCHOLOGY,
IN A DIRTY GARAGE,
I DO "PROJECT MASSAGE,"
BODIES LYING EVERYWHERE:
A PORNO COLLAGE!
GET THE ANSWER NOW.
   Alice.
I DID HYPNOSIS,
EIGHTY BUCKS A NEUROSIS!
   Sherry.
MEDITATION,
   Alice.
JUDO,
   Sherry.
AND SHIATSU,
   Alice.
SCIENTOLOGY,
   Sherry.
I DO ROLFING MONDAY NIGHTS,
AND TUESDAY IS ASTROLOGY.
   Alice.
FOODAHOLICS IS GREAT
BUT I JUST GOT MORE STODGY,
SO THEN AT LAST I DID A FAST
WITH THE GURU MAHARAJI!
   Sherry.
GET THE ANSWER, NOW!
   Gwen.
MY SON DID "NIETZCHE BUDDHISM",
AND NOW IT'S "JEWS FOR JESUS",
HE CAN'T UNDERSTAND WHY WE'RE UPSET,
HE THINKS RELIGION SHOULD PLEASE US.
HE SMILES ALL DAY WITH THIS LOOK OF ELATION.

I CAN'T KEEP RUNNING IN PLACE

(GWEN *stares off into space, eyes wide open, huge smile.*)
  ALICE.
I WAS LEARNING ITALIAN,
SO I SAVED UP FOR ROME,
I BOUGHT A MANTRA INSTEAD,
NOW I'VE LEARNED TO SAY "OHM,"
OHM OHM OHM, OHM OHM OHM,
I'D PREFER MY VACATION.
  SHERRY.
PSYCHODRAMA,
  ALICE.
MIND-BENDERS,
  BETH.
(*Showing the cigarette in her hand.*)
AND EIGHT MONTHS OF SMOKE-ENDERS,
  ALICE.
"NAM NYO HO RENGAY KYO,"
I'M INTO ZEN,
A FRIEND I KNOW SAID I SHOULD GO,
SINCE CLASSES ARE FILLED WITH MEN.
  SHERRY.
JOIN UP AT EST,
FOR JUST FOUR HUNDRED DOLLARS,
PRIMAL THERAPY'S THREE GRAND,
NO WONDER EVERYONE HOLLERS!
BUT,
THOSE "IN THE KNOW" WILL JOIN.
  BETH.
ANY JOE SHMOE WILL JOIN.
  SHERRY.
"GET THE ANSWER NOW."

BETH. How is this group any different from the others?
MICHELLE. I don't know. Ask Sherry.
SHERRY. (*Slowly and thoughtfully.*) Well, it's just different. Yeah, really different. Wow.
BETH. Thank you, Sherry.
MANDY. (*Crossing to* SHERRY.) Sherry, you really should write an article about all the different groups that you've . . .
BETH. (*Purposely interrupts* MANDY.) Well, now, who's got something to roleplay? I do. O.K., Beth, since you volunteered, why don't you begin? Thanks, I'd like to. Well, in the past

weeks, I've been furious with Carl because Carl has a habit of storing urine in the refrigerator. Not just anyone's urine, mind you, but the urine from the twenty-eight boys in the tenth grade class at Our Lady of Sorrow High School. It's an experiment Carl has been working on for some time now ... I guess you could say that Carl's hobby at the moment is piss. He got inspired several months ago at a medical convention of periodontists—a meeting of the gum gods—and now he's using urine as a way to detect certain types of gum diseases. Anyway, I suddenly got fed up with having my Frigidaire stocked full of twenty some-odd vials of parochial piss. And last night, instead of being assertive like a good girl and telling Carl how I feel, I decided to take it out on him. I made him some homemade soup. (EILEEN *looks as if she is about to gag.*) No, I didn't do what you're thinking. That would have been rather inelegant. Someone play Carl. Sherry, come on, you be Carl.
SHERRY. Sure.
EILEEN. Two timer!
BETH. Now, now, Eileen. Just because Sherry plays John most of the time doesn't mean she shouldn't play Carl. Anyway, it's not a very demanding part—just grunt a lot.

(SHERRY *stands and comes to the role-playing area in the Center while* BETH *arranges the furniture so that she and* "CARL" *are facing one another as they would be at a supper table.*)

BETH. (*Continued.*) (*Softly to the women so that* "CARL" *does not hear.*) Hot soup. (BETH *stirs the imaginary soup.*) Very hot soup. (BETH *serves the soup to* "CARL" *at the table.* BETH *stands to the side and watches him taste it.* "CARL" *takes a taste.*)
SHERRY. (*Carl.*) (*Burning tongue.*) Ah! (BETH *intended this.*)
BETH. (*Calmly, with mock sympathy.*) It's hot. Take care. (*To* MICHELLE.) Phone please. (MICHELLE *points to* ALICE.)
ALICE. Brrrrrrrrrrrrrrrrrring, brrrrrrrrrrrrrrring, brrrrrring . . .
BETH. (*Looking straight at* "CARL," *and not budging.*) I've got it. (BETH *allows the "phone" to ring for seven times without getting up.* "CARL," *puzzled by his wife's behavior, gets up to answer the "phone" himself.* BETH, *however, quickly and gracefully picks up the receiver* (ALICE's *hand*) *just before* HE *can get to it.* "CARL" *grumbles and returns to the table as* HE *cannot understand his wife's actions.*) I said I've got it. Hello? Fine and you? (*Looks at* "CARL" *for a brief moment.*) No. Certainly will.

Goodbye. (BETH *hangs up, returns to her seat at the table, looks at* "CARL", *and smiles sweetly.*) It's for you.
SHERRY. You didn't!
BETH. I sure as hell did.
SHERRY. Is Carl that bad?
ALICE. Yeah, really.
SHERRY. Nobody's that bad.
GWEN. You'd be surprised.
SHERRY. Beth, sometimes I think you exaggerate.
BETH. Yes . . . I do tend to see Carl through rose colored glasses.
MANDY. Someone's being evasive.
BETH. Someone's being obnoxious.
EILEEN. Beth.
BETH. So now everyone's playing shrink? Well, school's out, and I'd like to get home at a respectable hour. (*Gets up to leave.*)
MICHELLE. (*Sharply.*) Sit down, Beth. (*A long pause.* BETH *does not move.*) (*Softer, controlled.*) Please. (BETH *stalks back to her seat.*)
MICHELLE. (*Lightly.*) For next week's assignment I'd like each of you to make out a list of past honors, awards, prizes, anything like that at all.
GWEN. Do you accept short lists?
MICHELLE. Don't . . .
ALL. Put yourself down! (*The* WOMEN *laugh.*)
MICHELLE. That's all. Goodnight everyone. Have a good week. (*Ad libs "Goodnight", "See you next week"* . . .)
ALICE. Hey, Sherry, wanna get a bite?
SHERRY. Great. See you next week, guys. (ALICE *and* SHERRY *exit.* MANDY *is disturbed* SHE *has not been invited.* SHE *exits.* MICHELLE *goes to her desk to work, when* BETH *emerges from the entryway.*)
BETH. I thought I'd stay and we'd talk.
MICHELLE. (*Cautiously.*) Oh. What's on your mind?
BETH. You did the place yourself?
MICHELLE. Yes.
BETH. It's very brave.
MICHELLE. I've heard it called a lot of things. Never brave. Are you putting me on?
BETH. No. The color is very definite. Bold. Brave. My house is very pastel. Why'd you think I was putting you on?
MICHELLE. You're very tongue in cheek.

BETH. (*Overlapping.*) ... in cheek. Yes. There's probably a hole in my cheek by now. (*Pause.*) What's it like, living alone?
MICHELLE. I think you asked me that once before.
BETH. But we're by ourselves now. It's frightening, isn't it?
MICHELLE. No. It's exhilarating. My work is very important to me. Why? (BETH *starts to get her things.*)
BETH. Oh ... curiosity.
MICHELLE. (*Realizes.*) You're thinking of leaving Carl, aren't you? (BETH *nods.*) Beth, you should give it time.
BETH. Time? What do you call being married 20 years and being miserable for ten of them? Half-time?
MICHELLE. That's not giving it time. That's waiting it out. Like waiting for a terminal patient to die.
BETH. Lovely.
MICHELLE. (*Crosses to* BETH.) I'm not saying you shouldn't leave him. I'm just warning you ... advising you to give it every chance you can before you do. Don't be in such a hurry to throw it all away. You might be very sorry later. And it won't be easy on your daughter. Children can feel rejected.
BETH. (*Gently, thinking* MICHELLE *is opening up.*) I guess that's something you would understand.
MICHELLE. (*Defensively.*) What do you mean?
BETH. (*Taken aback.*) Well, I ... You're a psychologist, aren't you?
MICHELLE. (*Suddenly gets up, becoming distant, aloof.*) Oh, yes. Yes, I do see that in a lot of cases.
BETH. (*Annoyed.*) I think I had better be on my way.
MICHELLE. Yes ... It's been nice talking. (*Awkward silence as* BETH *puts on coat.*)
MICHELLE. Give some thought to what I said.
BETH. Next week is the last session.
MICHELLE. Yes, I know. (*Dismissing her.*) Good night.
BETH. (*Angry, but controlled, imitating* MICHELLE's *inflection.*) Good night. (BETH *exits, closing the door loudly.*) (MICHELLE *goes to phone, hesitates, then dials.*)
MICHELLE. Mark. It's me. I need to talk to you about Russell. Are you sure you didn't say something to him that might have ... My lawyer? No, not yet. I don't see why there's any reason to rush into ... (*Pause.*) Oh. I see ... Have the children met her? Uh huh. Fine. (*Weakly.*) Yes, all right. I said all right. I'll speak to him this week. Good bye. (MICHELLE *hangs up phone and tries to work at desk. Music begins and stops.* SHE *tries to work. Music begins and stops. Once again she attempts to work.*

Music begins again and continues. SHE *finally gives in to her thoughts.*)

"WHAT IF WE"

MICHELLE.
WHAT IF I HAD BEEN MORE PATIENT?
WHAT IF HE HAD LISTENED MORE?
WHAT IF WE HAD TRIED HARDER
BEFORE WE SHUT THE DOOR ON A LIFETIME?

WHAT IF I HAD BEEN MORE SUBTLE?
WHAT IF HE HAD BEEN MORE CARING?
WHAT IF WE HAD TRIED JUST A LITTLE HARDER
BEFORE WE GAVE UP SHARING A LIFETIME?

QUESTIONS DANGLE FROM THE CEILING
AS I LIE AWAKE,
WONDERING "WHAT IF? WHAT IF?
WHAT IF WE MADE A MISTAKE?"

WHAT IF WE HAD BEEN MORE GIVING?
WHAT IF WE HAD LISTENED MORE?
WHAT IF WE HAD TRIED HARDER
BEFORE WE SHUT THE DOOR ON A LIFETIME?

SO WHAT IF I'M ALONE!
SO WHAT IF HE'S NOT HERE!
SO WHAT IF THERE ARE SHADOWS
THAT WILL NEVER DISAPPEAR . . .
SO WHAT!
SO WHAT!
SO WHAT . . . IF?

ACT TWO

SCENE 2

THE LAST SESSION, IN PROGRESS

EILEEN. (*Looking around the circle.*) I've been waiting for Wednesday night all week. Well . . . I did it. I told John how I feel. About everything. It took me about fifteen rehearsals, pretending John was the calendar, or the wall clock or mirror or the bed post . . . And then there came a moment when I knew I could do it. I was looking the Mixmaster right in the eye. I left the kitchen and found John reading in the living room. And he listened. He listened to me for as long as I spoke, about twenty-five minutes straight without interrupting me. And John and I have arranged it so that I'll be out two nights and also two afternoons a week so I can go back to school.

MICHELLE. Bravo!
ALICE. Incredible.
SHERRY. Aren't you proud of yourself?
EILEEN. Yes! Michelle, thank you. (ALL *except* BETH *share in* EILEEN'S *excitement;* BETH *is seated apart from the other* WOMEN.)
GWEN. You mean he didn't rant and rave?
EILEEN. No.
GWEN. Not at all?
EILEEN. No, John wasn't half as unwilling as I thought he'd be. In fact, once I explained how I felt, he was actually encouraging.
GWEN. But what about all your kids?
EILEEN. We'll get a sitter. (GWEN *appears baffled.*)
MICHELLE. That really is wonderful, I'm proud of you. (WOMEN *ad lib "congratulations," etc.*) Alice, do you have anything *you'd* like to talk about?
ALICE. Me? Nah.
MICHELLE. It's the last session. There must be something you'd like to share.
ALICE. I've got some Fig Newtons. (ALL *of the* WOMEN, *except* MICHELLE, *laugh aloud at* ALICE'S *jokes.*)
MICHELLE. Can't you take yourself seriously for one moment?
ALICE. I try not to.
MICHELLE. Alice, what are you interested in doing?
ALICE. You mean, what am I going to do when I grow up? And shrink down?
MICHELLE. Is that a goal?
ALICE. (*Uncomfortable.*) Not particularly. Hey, what do you call it when you can't resist a chocolate cream pie that's baking in the oven and so you run into the kitchen, pull open the oven door, take out the cake before the normal cooking time and cut yourself a huge piece?
SHERRY. What?

ALICE. A bavarian section!
MICHELLE. I bet you're a dynamite performer.
ALICE. I am.
MICHELLE. Then why aren't you working now?
ALICE. I couldn't find a producer that was willing to pay both of me.
MICHELLE. Alice! (*Pause.*) Why don't you want to act anymore?
ALICE. Who said that?
SHERRY. Michelle, it's not that easy to get acting work. I was talking with some actors . . .
ALICE. I worked. In the same week, ABC signed me for a new soap and I got the second lead in the national tour of . . .
SHERRY. Wow. Which soap? I bet I saw you.
ALICE. Hey, what's the difference between the fat lady at the circus and the . . .
MICHELLE. Alice.
ALICE. Yeah?
MICHELLE. Why didn't you do the show?
ALICE. I don't know. All of a sudden I was signing things and I was getting paid a lot of money and there were demands being put on me . . .
BETH. It's called pressure.
MICHELLE. (*To* BETH.) It's called success.
SHERRY. What do you mean?
MICHELLE. Did you work after that?
ALICE. Well, I got cast in something down in Washington.
MICHELLE. And?
ALICE. I didn't show up for rehearsal.
MICHELLE. Why not?
ALICE. I like doing nothing. It's mind expanding.
SHERRY. Like meditation.
ALICE. Yeah, right. My life is one big "Ohm."
MICHELLE. What are you afraid of Alice?
ALICE. I didn't say I was afraid of anything.
MICHELLE. You know best.
ALICE. Please don't do that.
MICHELLE. What?
ALICE. "You know best." My parents pull that all the time.
MICHELLE. They don't find your lifestyle mind expanding?
ALICE. I embarrass them. Ya know. "PRETTY GIRL WITH TALENT GETS FAT, RUINS LIFE."
MICHELLE. Is your mother overweight?

ALICE. Are you kidding? She makes Twiggy look like Winston Churchill. (*As usual, several* WOMEN *laugh at* ALICE's *joke.*)

SHERRY. Wow.

ALICE. They're embarrassed, all right.

EILEEN. They're concerned for you.

ALICE. Well, it's my life, right?

MICHELLE. Is it?

ALICE. What?

MICHELLE. Are you really in control of it? (ALICE *shrugs.*) It's one thing to be assertive and confront other people and another to be able to confront yourself.

ALICE. Isn't that a movie with Cary Grant? (No ONE *laughs.*) I'm losing my touch. (*The Phone rings.*)

MICHELLE. Mandy, would you please get that? (MANDY *answers phone.*)

MANDY. It's your husband, Gwen.

MICHELLE. Alice, I have an idea for a scene I'd like you to do. (GWEN, *however, has the* WOMEN's *attention.*)

GWEN. (*Unaware that she is audible.*) Hello? Well, how about the glove compartment? All right, dear. But please hurry. Please.

MICHELLE. Alice, there's a scene I want you to try.

ALICE. Why? (MICHELLE *gives her a look.*) All right already! Anyway, I haven't been cast this much in ages.

MICHELLE. You play your mother.

ALICE. (*Not particularly pleased.*) Oh.

MICHELLE. Is that agreeable?

ALICE. Yeah. It'll be a good dry run for the role of Queen Elizabeth.

MICHELLE. And who should play Alice?

ALICE. A raving beauty, of course.

MICHELLE. Mandy, how about you?

MANDY. No. (*Pause.*) I can't get into that type of thing.

MICHELLE. I don't want to push anyone. If I have to play her myself I will . . . (*Standing up.*)

BETH. Mandy, why don't you surprise everyone and do something nice for a change?

EILEEN. (*Cut it out.*) Beth.

GWEN. Are you sure you looked under the pingpong table? You were working there last night. Well, I'm sorry but it's Wednesday night.

MICHELLE. Here's the situation. (*To* ALICE.) You're playing your mother. (GWEN *continues to have the* WOMEN's *attention.*)

GWEN. You're right, Dear. My coat is already on. Goodbye. (*As* GWEN *enters, the* WOMEN *look up.*) No, no. Don't stop. I'm afraid I've got to go. Really. Please don't let me interrupt.

MICHELLE. Is there a problem?

GWEN. Nothing serious. My littlest one has the flu and he's feeling awfully sick, so I really have to go.

MICHELLE. Gwen, please don't leave. We'll be through in a little while.

GWEN. (*Putting on jacket.*) I know, but I do have to go.

EILEEN. Gwen, it's the last class.

GWEN. Right. (*Sighs.*) Well, if I find the—(*Catches herself.*) If I find that he's not as sick as all that, I'll come right back.

MICHELLE. I hope we'll see you.

GWEN. Me too.

SHERRY. I hope he feels better.

GWEN. Yeah. (*Pause.*) Thanks. (GWEN *is about to close the door behind her.*)

MANDY. Why are you going home?

GWEN. My boy Larry is sick.

MANDY. Why are you going home, Gwen?

GWEN. I told you . . .

MANDY. You're afraid of your husband. Why'd you have to lie to us? (GWEN *looks fleetingly at the* GROUP *and exits Left.* MANDY *calls down the stairs after her.*)

MANDY. I can't believe you're leaving. Why are you afraid of us? (*Door downstairs heard closing.*)

BETH. (*To* MANDY.) You little bitch!

SHERRY. Why'd you have to go and do that? I mean, like she felt bad enough.

MANDY. (*To* MICHELLE.) Why'd you let her get away with that?

BETH. Get away with what? You think she wanted to go home? You think she wasn't humiliated enough?

SHERRY. Maybe he lost something important.

MANDY. She lied. She could have confided in us.

BETH. You think it would have made a difference? I've confided in this group a lot and my life hasn't changed in the slightest. But at least I realize I'm never going to get anywhere. Which is more than I can say for the rest of you.

EILEEN. I think you're being unfair.

BETH. Look, what else is this but menopausal babysitting?

SHERRY. I'm not menopausal.

BETH. And this is so much better than night school at the Y.

Because here we really get the *impression* that we're getting somewhere.

EILEEN. Beth!

BETH. (*To* MICHELLE.) She has us doing so much psychological huffing and puffing, we hardly realize that we're running in place.

EILEEN. How can you say that?

ALICE. Yeah, really.

BETH. Push pull click click. Change your life this quick. Get the answer now!

SHERRY. (*Crosses to* BETH.) Oh, please don't start. We always got along so well and it's the last time we're going to be together.

BETH. All right, Smiley. What gold stars have you earned on *your* progress chart?

SHERRY. Where are you coming from Beth? Gee.

BETH. Well?

SHERRY. (*Slowly, thoughtfully, undefensively.*) Well, for one, I would say that I am almost ready to talk to Mike about making some changes in the way we relate.

EILEEN. Maybe you are at the point of breaking through to something, Beth.

ALICE. Like things are just beginning to happen for me this week. Perhaps it's just a matter of time for you.

BETH. Almost ready to talk with Mike. Maybe there will be a breakthrough. Perhaps we all just need some time. Almost, maybe, perhaps. Almost, maybe, perhaps. Listen to yourselves with your almosts, maybes, and perhapses. Sounds like something I could waltz to if I were a cripple. Wake up ladies. You're in a psychological massage parlor, and it feels so good, you've fallen asleep on the table. Wake up! You don't want to miss the three course banquet included in the deal.

ALICE. I don't know what good you think you're doing by . . .

BETH. Don't worry, Alice. It's all non-caloric. Just sit back and relax while—(*To* MICHELLE.) our hostess serves us the almosts, maybes, and perhapses.

(*MUSIC.*)

"ALMOSTS, MAYBES, AND PERHAPSES"

BETH.
IT'S A SITDOWN AFFAIR,
FOR TEN BUCKS A PLATE,

BUT WHAT DO YOU CARE?
IT'S NOT A BAD RATE.
IT'S AN EVENING TO PRETEND
THAT TOMORROW YOU INTEND
TO BE WHAT YOU WANT TO BE.

FOR LADIES WITH NOTHING
TO SHOW FOR THEMSELVES,
GALS NOT ON THE GO,
PUT THESE ON YOUR SHELVES!
THEY'RE WHAT YOU NEED!
THEY'RE GUARANTEED!
TO TAKE AWAY THE BITTER AFTERTASTE,
FROM A LIFE OF WASTE.

ALMOSTS, MAYBES, AND PERHAPSES.
ALMOSTS, MAYBES, AND PERHAPSES.

YOU'RE ALMOST THERE!
 Sherry. Right!
 Beth.
MAYBE YOU'LL WIN.
 Eileen. Yes!
 Beth.
PERHAPS YOU CAN CHANGE!
 Alice. When I'm r . . .
 Beth.
READY CLASS? LET'S BEGIN!
IT'S AN EVENING TO PRETEND
THAT TOMORROW YOU INTEND
TO BE WHAT YOU WANT TO BE.

STIR FRY YOUR DREAMS
'TIL THEY'RE NONDESCRIPT.
ALLOW THEM TO SETTLE
FOR TEN YEARS OR MORE.
ADD SOME TEARS, STIR LIKE BEFORE,
MIX IN THE MAYBES,
THE ALMOSTS,
ADD A DASH OF PERHAPSES!

TOMORROW NIGHT WHEN YOU'RE DEPRESSED,
YOU CAN HAVE A BITE OF THE REST
OF WEDNESDAY'S LEFTOVER LIES.

ALMOSTS, MAYBES, AND PERHAPSES.
ALMOSTS, MAYBES, AND PERHAPSES.
ALMOSTS, MAYBES, AND PERHAPSES.

IT'S A SITDOWN AFFAIR,
FOR TEN BUCKS A PLATE,
BUT WHAT DO YOU CARE?
IT'S NOT A BAD RATE,
IT'S AN EVENING TO PRETEND
THAT TOMORROW YOU INTEND
TO BE WHAT YOU WANT TO BE.

FOR LADIES WITH NOTHING
TO SHOW FOR THEMSELVES,
GALS NOT ON THE GO,
PUT THESE ON YOUR SHELVES.
THEY'RE WHAT YOU NEED!
THEY'RE GUARANTEED!
TO TAKE AWAY THE BITTER AFTERTASTE
FROM A LIFE OF WASTE.

LIFE ONCE WAS DOLEFUL
BUT NOW LIFE'S A BOWLFUL
OF ALMOSTS, MAYBES, AND PERHAPSES,
YOUR SPIRITS WILL RISE,
OVERSTUFFED WITH YOUR LIES,
AS YOU SHUT YOUR EYES
AND YOUR DREAM COLLAPSES!

YOU'RE ALMOST THERE.
MAYBE YOU'LL WIN.
PERHAPS YOU CAN CHANGE,
READY CLASS? LET'S BEGIN.
IT'S AN EVENING TO PRETEND
THAT TOMORROW WE INTEND
TO BE WHAT WE WANT,
TO BE WHAT WE WANT,
TO BE WHAT WE WANT TO BE.

ALMOSTS, MAYBES, AND PERHAPSES,
ALMOSTS, MAYBES, AND PERHAPSES,
ALMOSTS, MAYBES, AND PERHAPSES.

I CAN'T KEEP RUNNING IN PLACE

I AM AN ALMOST DOCTOR.
I AM AN ALMOST GOOD WIFE.
I HAVE AN ALMOST GOOD MARRIAGE,
I HAD AN ALMOST GOOD LIFE.

MICHELLE. I'm sorry you feel that way Beth.

BETH. I should have known, those who can't do, teach.

SHERRY. Like, what's that supposed to mean?

EILEEN. I resent your talking for the whole group. Michelle saved my marriage.

MICHELLE. No I didn't. You did, Eileen. You made the effort.

BETH. I see. Beth gets a D for effort. Look, I laid my whole Peyton Place on the table.

MICHELLE. But you never took the next step. Did you ever once try to discuss your needs with Carl? Or with your daughter? No, you come here and amuse everyone with your glib remarks.

BETH. That's enough.

MICHELLE. Are you leaving Carl?

BETH. What does that have to do . . .

MICHELLE. I asked you something. Are you leaving your husband?

BETH. Yes.

MICHELLE. And you mean to tell me that that decision has nothing to do with the group? Answer me.

BETH. I said that's enough.

MICHELLE. I'm leading this group.

BETH. Don't push me.

MICHELLE. If you can't get your life together, don't blame me. Some of the women here find my council very helpful.

BETH. Your council? Why should any of us follow your council, may I ask? So we can all be "free" and end up like you? You work your buns off running these groups because you're too proud to take money from your husband, am I right? I bet if a man were to come along right now and say "jump" you'd ask how high. You're free all right. And all alone and pretty damned confused about breaking up your own marriage. It kills you that we still have our families. You can't stand the fact that we still have a place where we are unappreciated and abused.

SHERRY. Michelle, don't listen to her. She's just all mixed-up and middle-aged.

ALICE. Really, Michelle. I've learned a lot from you.

EILEEN. Me, too.

MICHELLE. Thank you, but there is no need for testimonials. I'm a big girl. You have no right to call me a phony. I left my marriage because I wanted the chance to work at my career. To help people like you. Of course I miss my children. I want them with me. But I want to be able to support them, myself. And I was happy about my decision because I knew what I wanted and . . . I was assertive about changing my life. (SHE *is breaking down.*) I knew . . . I knew what I wanted and I . . . excuse me . . . (MICHELLE *exits into other part of loft, offstage.* SHE *returns moments later, after the* GROUP *has endured a long silence.*) Shall we give it a go again? You're playing your mother and . . .

MANDY. And I'm playing Alice.

BETH. Well, well.

MICHELLE. (*Touched.*) Thank you, Mandy. I'm sure Alice appreciates it.

ALICE. (*Unenthused.*) Yeah, really. Thanks.

MANDY. Let's just start, O.K.? (ALICE *and* MANDY *face each other in the role-playing area.*)

MICHELLE. Let's set up the scene. Your mother comes to visit you and she's trying to convince you to get your act together, all right?

ALICE. We don't have to do this now. She's coming over tomorrow night.

MANDY. Hello, Mother.

ALICE. (*As her Jewish mother.*) Alice, hello, dahling.

MANDY. Well, come in already.

ALICE. Mandy, I'd be glad to see her. You can be nicer.

BETH. Don't be so demanding, Alice. It's hard for Mandy to be nice.

MICHELLE. Beth. If you have something constructive to say, then participate in the exercise.

BETH. Yeah, yeah.

MANDY. (*To* MICHELLE.) All right?

MICHELLE. Yes, please continue.

MANDY. Please do come in.

ALICE. Mandy, I wouldn't be so formal, ya know?

MANDY. All right, all right. (*To* MICHELLE.) I told you I wasn't good at this.

MICHELLE. You're doing fine.

MANDY. Hey, ma, how's it hanging?

MICHELLE. Come on.

MANDY. Hello, how are you?
ALICE. Don't ask. But more important, how are *you*?
MANDY. Fine.
ALICE. How's your diet?
MANDY. I've been cheating.
ALICE. No, I'd say, "She's fine, and she sends you her regards."
MANDY. She's fine, and she sends you her regards.
ALICE. Dahling, when are you going to grow up?
MANDY. Leave off, will you?
ALICE. I can't. You think it's easy for us to watch you eat yourself into a hole?
MANDY. I'm not in a hole, thank you.
ALICE. Would you get down off your fat horse. No, that's not fair, she wouldn't say that. Let me see. It hurts us to see you so unhappy.
MANDY. I'm not unhappy, thank you. (MICHELLE *crosses to* ALICE, *stands behind her, facing* MANDY. MICHELLE *rests her hand lightly on* ALICE'S *shoulder.*)
MICHELLE. Why can't you be honest with yourself?
MANDY. Are you calling me a liar?
MICHELLE. You're running away from yourself. You're afraid of trying because you're afraid of failing. School plays were terrific because everyone patted you on the back, and now it's the big time and you're scared.
MANDY. Yeah?
MICHELLE. Yeah! And maybe being fat keeps you away from men. No one can hurt you cause no one will come near you. And not just because you're fat. But because you're so defensive, even if a man liked you he couldn't have a normal conversation with you.
MANDY. That's not so.
MICHELLE. Come on, Alice. You're a one-woman vaudeville act.
EILEEN. (*As* ALICE.) But tell me what to do. I don't know where to start.
MICHELLE. You can start by being honest with yourself.
ALICE. You can start by being honest with yourself.
MANDY. Leave off.
ALICE. And it's time you learned to trust someone.
MANDY. I do.

ALICE. Yeah, Sarah Lee.
MANDY. Can't you think of anything else to talk about? Jesus, are you ever boring.
BETH. (*Steps into role-playing area and addresses* MANDY.) I am, am I?
EILEEN. (*Still as* ALICE.) No, Mom, I'm sorry I said . . .
MANDY. (*To* BETH.) Will you please stay out of this?
BETH. No.
ALICE. (*Still as her mother.*) When are you going to trust someone?
MANDY. (*Trying to focus on playing* ALICE.) Don't tell me what to do.
BETH. You can't trust anyone, because you can't be trusted yourself.
MANDY. (*To* BETH *from now on.*) Don't start with me!
BETH. Don't you threaten me, young lady.
MANDY. Why not?
BETH. I am tired of being treated this way, do you understand? I deserve some respect.
MANDY. Earn it.
BETH. How dare you.
SHERRY. Everyone's so serious . . .

(*From this point on,* MANDY *tells* BETH *what she has wanted to tell her step-mother, and* BETH *tells* MANDY *what she has wanted to express to her own daughter.*)

MANDY. Why do you hate me?
SHERRY. We're all such good friends.
BETH. I don't hate you, for God's sake.
SHERRY. Stop it.
MANDY. I wanted you to like me. I've tried.
BETH. You have not.
MANDY. And we are so damn polite.
BETH. Is that so?
MANDY. Yes.
SHERRY. Hey, you guys!
BETH. Is that what you call polite? Disappointing me at the last minute?
MANDY. I disappoint *you?* *You're* the one who's hung a "Do not disturb" sign all over you.
BETH. You couldn't spend one week with your mother.

I CAN'T KEEP RUNNING IN PLACE

MANDY. Since when did you ever want to spend time with me?
BETH. What? I've given up everything for you.
MANDY. What a laugh. And if you're going to start calling yourself my mother, then act like one!
SHERRY. Shhh!
BETH. You will respect me like you respect your father!
MANDY. I love my father.
BETH. What about me? You don't appreciate all that I've . . .
MANDY. All that bullshit you call affection? No. No thank you, I don't appreciate your stupid gifts. You don't give a damn about me. Like that time I was sick and I called home? Daddy was away—but you were there—with your card game. You couldn't even come to the phone. No, you sent your maid over with throat lozenges. And the name of your Doctor—well *SHIT!* All I wanted was a "Hello, Mandy, how are you feeling?" (SHE *is breaking down.*) All I wanted was . . . (BETH *takes a step toward* MANDY *and embraces her.*)
BETH. All I want is to be allowed to love you. (*A long pause.* EILEEN *takes* MANDY *from* BETH *and brings her back to her seat.* SHERRY *is in tears.* BETH *remains standing.* ALICE *takes her seat.*) (*Long pause.*) I'm sorry. I really . . . (*To* MICHELLE.) I really am sorry. (*Silence hangs over* THE GROUP. MICHELLE *crosses to* MANDY, *embraces her. After a moment,* GWEN *enters.*)
GWEN. The door was open. I . . . (GWEN *crosses to the group.*) I never went home. I've been sitting in the car. This was my one night out and he didn't care. He knew I would be humiliated and he didn't care. I left here for a slide rule. To get down on my hands and knees and look under every bed and mull through every garbage can to see if a fifteen year old slide rule was accidentally thrown out. I've spent twenty years searching for other people's things. I won't do that anymore. (*Ad libs from* THE WOMEN *of "congratulations," "I'm so glad you're here," etc. Suddenly,* GWEN *senses that* SHE *has missed something that has transpired in the* GROUP.)
MICHELLE. That's a good first step.
GWEN. I hope so.
MANDY. (*Crossing to* GWEN.) I'm really sorry I did that.
GWEN. Don't be. It's the reason I came back. (THEY *embrace.*)
MANDY. Alice, listen, I'm sorry I stole your scene.
ALICE. It's the first time I ever let anyone upstage me. Really, it's O.K.

EILEEN. Anyway, Mandy, if there's anything Alice wants to work on, she can do it next Wednesday night . . .
SHERRY. Wow.
GWEN. I know.
ALICE. I hadn't even thought about it really.
BETH. I've been thinking about it all evening.
EILEEN. I can't believe this is the last session.
MICHELLE. In fact, it's late. We've run over.
MANDY. It's really . . .
SHERRY. Kinda strange.

(*MUSIC begins; the flute recalls the theme of the opening song as* MICHELLE *crosses to each* WOMAN. *Every goodbye is individual and reflects* MICHELLE'S *relationship to that particular woman. The last she approaches is* BETH. MICHELLE *then crosses upstage and speaks to the group.*)

MICHELLE. It's going to be difficult to break away. If you want, you can exchange addresses and phone numbers, but most likely you won't see anyone from this workshop again. Maybe—on a street. In a store. But never in the way we know each other now.
WOMEN. BUT IF I'M FORTY-TWO . . . (EACH *says her own age.*)
MICHELLE. We've been a kind of life-support system for each other in these past six weeks.
WOMEN.
DON'T KNOW WHO I AM,
WHAT'S A SIX-WEEK CRASH COURSE GOING TO SHOW ME?
MICHELLE. And we'll continue to be that for each other.
WOMEN.
TELL THESE STRANGERS MY PROBLEMS,
WHY SHOULD THEY GIVE A DAMN?
MICHELLE. But only in the sense that each of us knows that we'll be rooting for one another.
WOMEN.
AND I'M NOT SURE I REALLY WANT THEM TO KNOW ME.
MICHELLE. Especially after tonight,
WOMEN.
ALL THESE FACES I SEE,

I CAN'T KEEP RUNNING IN PLACE 77

THEY'RE JUST WOMEN LIKE ME . . .

MICHELLE. Each of us will have to root for herself. (MICHELLE *motions for the* WOMEN *to form a trust circle. It is the same trust excercise* THEY *did in the first session. The relaxed, close feeling in the* GROUP *is totally different from the tension experienced the first time the exercise was executed in the first session.* EACH *takes her turn in the center, falling back with total trust into the arms of the other* WOMEN.)

"WHERE WILL I BE NEXT WEDNESDAY NIGHT?"

(*As the* WOMEN *cross downstage to form the trust circle.*)

MANDY.
WHERE WILL I BE NEXT WEDNESDAY NIGHT? (MANDY *falls into circle.*)
SHERRY.
WEDNESDAY NIGHT IS MY FRIEND.
EILEEN.
I COULD ALWAYS DEPEND ON WEDNESDAY NIGHT.
GWEN.
I FORGOT THAT THE FRIENDSHIP WOULD END.

(GWEN *enters the circle and falls, then returns to her place. During the vamp,* SHERRY *enters the circle. She falls once, then takes a relaxed deep breath and falls again.*)

MICHELLE.
WHERE WILL I BE NEXT WEDNESDAY NIGHT?
BETH.
I HAVEN'T ANY PLAN.
ALICE.
WILL MY NEW AGENDA PAGE STAY WHITE?
ALL.
WILL I CHOOSE WHAT I WANT NEXT WEDNESDAY NIGHT?
(BETH *falls into circle.*)
WHERE WILL I BE NEXT WEDNESDAY NIGHT?
WHO WILL I BE NEXT WEDNESDAY NIGHT? (EILEEN *falls into the circle.*)
(*During the musical passage,* ALICE *enters the circle and falls, this time successfully. Finally,* MICHELLE *falls back*

into the circle. As the WOMEN *lift* MICHELLE *from the fall, the MUSIC suddenly quickens.*)

MICHELLE.
I KNOW WHERE YOU'LL BE NEXT WEDNESDAY NIGHT.
YOU WON'T BE STRANDED ON THAT CORNER OF FIFTH AND SELF-DOUBT.
YOU'LL BE STRIDING DOWN THAT AVENUE
I NOW SEE STRETCHED OUT
BEFORE YOU.
 EILEEN.
I'LL BE CONFIDENT,
 GWEN.
I'LL BE STRONG.
 BETH.
THEY'LL SAY I'M SINGING OFF KEY,
 ALICE.
I'LL SAY I'M SINGING MY SONG.
 SHERRY.
I'LL BE CONFIDENT,
 MANDY.
I'LL BE STRONG.
 ALL.
THEY'LL SAY I'M SINGING OFF KEY.
I'LL SAY I'M SINGING MY SONG.

(*The above develops into a round.*)

(*With sudden insecurity.*)
 BETH AND ALICE.
I'LL BE . . .
 MANDY AND SHERRY.
I'LL BE . . .
 EILEEN AND GWEN.
THEY'LL SAY I'M . . .
 MICHELLE.
I'LL SAY I'M . . .
 GWEN.
BUT THERE'S MY HUSBAND WHO TELLS ME THAT HE NEEDS ME AT HOME.
 ALICE.

THERE'S A FRIGHTENING FEELING THAT I'LL STAY WHERE I AM.
  BETH.
THERE'S A DAUGHTER WHO'S BECOMING WHAT I'LL NEVER BE.
  MICHELLE.
THERE'S MY BLUE-EYED SON WHO REFUSES TO SEE ME.
  SHERRY.
THERE'S AN EMPTINESS I CAN'T SEEM TO FILL.
  MANDY.
THERE'S A MOTHER I'VE NEEDED WHO'S LEFT ME ALONE.
  EILEEN.
THERE IS WORK I'M AFRAID TO BEGIN.
  ALL.
WHERE WILL I BE NEXT WEDNESDAY NIGHT?
WHERE WILL I BE?

BLACKOUT.

I CAN'T KEEP RUNNING IN PLACE

ACT I, Scene I

MICHELLE:
  Coral Tailored Jacket
  Grey Wool Slacks
  Grey Cotton Tank Top
  Coral and Grey Print Scarf
  Grey Shoes
BETH:
  Copen Blue Vest and Skirt
  Light Blue and Lavender Patterned Silk Blouse
  Grey Boots
  Grey Clutch Bag
EILEEN:
  Lavender Print Maternity Dress
  Tan Character Shoes
SHERRY:
  Bright Primary Striped Crocheted Sweater
  Cuffed Blue Jeans
  Red Rubber Wallabees/Blue Vinyl Sports bag
GWEN:
  Red Lacoste Turtleneck
  Rust and Purple Oversweater with Maroon Trim
  Designer Jeans
  Brown Boots
ALICE:
  Bright Yellow/Green Pants
  Red/Green/Yellow Plaid Big Shirt
  Red Glitter Scarf
  Lavender Cowboy Boots
  Blue Knee Socks/Maroon Cloth Bag
MANDY:
  Navy Blue Monogrammed Pullover
  Maroon Jeans
  Topsiders
  Maroon and White Socks/Dark Blue Book Bag

ACT I, Scene 2
(Later that Evening)

MICHELLE:
  Maroon Velour Bathrobe

ACT I, Scene 3

MICHELLE:
  Maroon Silk Blouse
  Grey Tank Top
  Grey Wool Slacks
  Red/Brown Shoes
BETH:
  Violet Dolman Sleeved Jersey Dress
  Gold Plate Link Belt
  Dark Stockings
  Brown T-Strap Shoes
  Wide Gold Bracelet/Gold Earrings
  Gold Shoulder Bar Pin
  Dark Brown Clutch Bag
  Designer Raincoat
EILEEN:
  Light Brown Tweed Man's Suit
  White Oxford Shirt
  Dark Brown and Orange Striped Tie
  Tan Character Shoes
SHERRY:
  Pink/Yellow/Sky Blue Plaid Jumper
  Matching Plaid Headband
  Sky Blue Peter Pan Collar Blouse
  Sea Blue Box Apron with Rickrack
  Pink Corduroy 'pregnant' pillow
  Light Stockings
  Pink Barettes
  Blue Denim Wedgies
GWEN:
  Maroon Indian Print Matching Blouse and Gypsy Skirt
  Bright Blue Beads
  Gold Chains
  Blue and Gold Bangle Bracelets
  Copen Blue Beret
  Black/Maroon/Gold Tie Belt with Fringe
  Large Gold Loop Earrings
  Brown Leather Boots
ALICE:
  Deep Aquagreen Raincoat
  Red Slipper Sandals

Bright Blue Gloves with Maribou Trim
Red Sunglasses
Rhinestone Loop Earrings
Sky Blue Big T-Shirt with Rhinestones and Fringe
Baby Blue Fringe Collar
Violet/Maroon Striped Metallic Harem Pants with Bangles
(in Bag) Light Blue Metallic Scarf
Red and Blue Feather Boa

MANDY:
    Light Grey Alpine Pullover with Snowflake Collar
    Maroon Jeans
    White Cotton Turtleneck
    Maroon and White Socks
    Topsiders
    Deep Blue Down Vest

ACT II, Scene I

MICHELLE:
    Black Linen Slacks
    Pink and Grey/Green Striped Shirt with Pink Trim
    Black Shoes
    Grey/Green Tie Belt

BETH:
    Light Pink Belted Jersey Dress with Collar
    Navy Blue Blazer
    String Pears
    Bone Sandals/Beige Clutch bag

EILEEN:
    Medium Blue Velour Jumper
    Blue/Rust/White Plaid Blouse
    Light Blue Paisley Scarf
    Tan Character Shoes

SHERRY:
    Red and White Hawaiian Print Shirt
    Purple Tank Top
    Wide Purple Cloth Belt
    Purple Safari Jeans
    Light Lavender Sneakers
    Purple/Orange/Green Bright Striped Socks

GWEN:
    Purple Silk Blouse

I CAN'T KEEP RUNNING IN PLACE

   Khaki Slacks
   Grey/Beige T-Strap Shoes
   Black Watch
ALICE:
   Yellow Tied Overalls
   Yellow and Red Striped Pullover Shirt
   Red Tie Shoes
   Grey Vest with Red Lining and Buttons
MANDY:
   Navy and White Plaid Oxford Shirt
   Light Blue Jeans
   Navy Cloth Belt
   Bright Blue Socks
   White and Blue Adidas

ACT II, Scene 2:

MICHELLE:
   Peach Silk Tunic with Black and Sky Blue Print
   Black Linen Slacks
   Black Shoes
BETH:
   Red Tie-Front Silk Dress with Flower Print Trim
   Bone Sandals
EILEEN:
   Tan Sport Shirt with White and Blue Stripe and Red Trim
   Tan Slacks
   Black Shoes
SHERRY:
   Yellow Gauze Embroidered Shirt with White Fringe
   White T-Shirt with Rose Applique
   Pale Yellow Jeans
   Deep Yellow Socks with Red Dots
   Mustard Chinese Slip-on Shoes
   Brown Belt
   Yellow Barettes
GWEN:
   Blue/Green/White Striped Tailored Shirt
   Lime Green Skirt
   Tan T-Strap Shoes
ALICE:
   Black Flower Print 30's-Style Dress with Turquoise Trim

Light Turquoise Slip-on Sandals
Pink Anklets
MANDY:
White Sport Shirt with Small Stripes
Light Blue Jeans
Navy Cloth Belt
Bright Blue Socks
White and Blue Adidas

UPSTAGE RIGHT ORCHESTRA GATE:
Pop-up Tissue Box
Ashtray
Various Potted Plants
Overhead Hanging Plants

PERSONAL PROPS:
BETH:
All Handbags preset with:
Gold Cigarette Lighter
Gold Cigarette Case
Cigarettes
Compact
Spare Matches
(I,2)-
Stethoscope
Bifocals
White Lab Coat
MICHELLE:
Watch with Black Band
MANDY:
Blue Bookbag
Notepad
Pen
SHERRY:
Vinyl Sports Bag
Brush (in Sports Bag)
(I,2)-
Blue Plastic Tray with:
Carrot Cake (frosted with lettering)
6 Blue Plastic Plates
6 Blue Paper Napkins
6 White Plastic Forks

Cake Server
　　Plastic Wrap (to cover tray)
　Red Rain Slicker
ALICE:
　Maroon Cloth Bag with:
　　Gum
　　Blush Compact
　　Feather Boa
　　Blue Metallic Scarf
EILEEN:
　Purse
　(I,2)-
　Briefcase
　Lightweight Overcoat
GWEN:
　Beige and Brown Purse
　(I,2)-
　Jacket
　(II,1)-
　Jacket

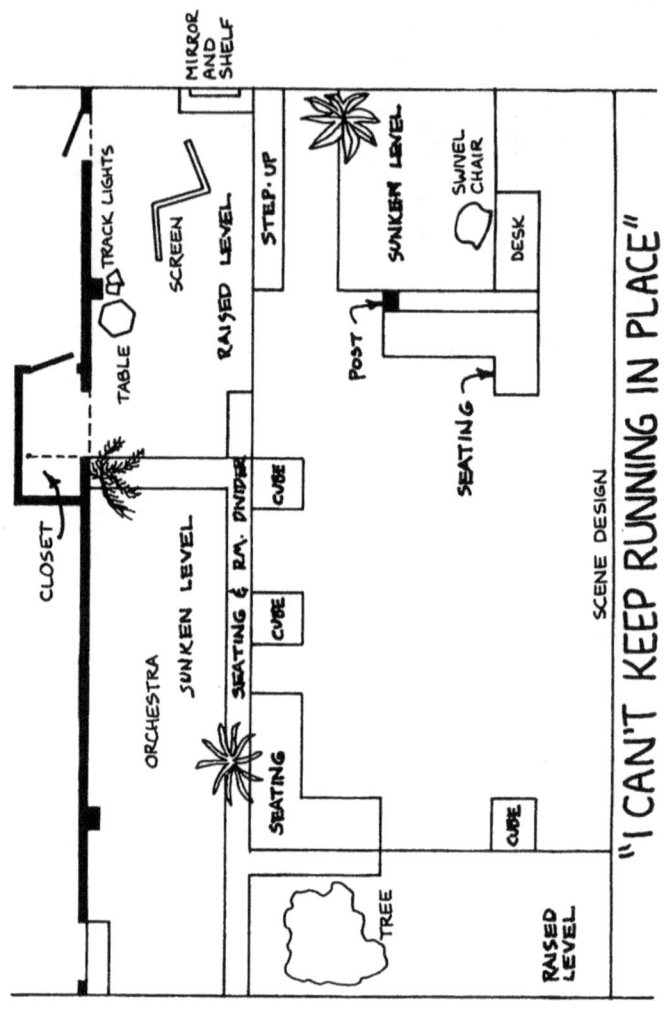

A licensing fee must be paid whether the title(s) is presented for charity or gain and whether or not admission is charged. Professional/Stock licensing fees are quoted upon application to Concord Theatricals Corp.

This work is published by Samuel French, an imprint of Concord Theatricals Corp.

No one shall make any changes in this title(s) for the purpose of production. No part of this book may be reproduced, stored in a retrieval system, scanned, uploaded, or transmitted in any form, by any means, now known or yet to be invented, including mechanical, electronic, digital, photocopying, recording, videotaping, or otherwise, without the prior written permission of the publisher. No one shall share this title(s), or any part of this title(s), through any social media or file hosting websites.

For all inquiries regarding motion picture, television, online/digital and other media rights, please contact Concord Theatricals Corp.

MUSIC AND THIRD PARTY MATERIALS USE NOTE

Licensees are solely responsible for obtaining formal written permission from copyright owners to use copyrighted music and/or other copyrighted third-party materials (e.g., artworks, logos) in the performance of this play and are strongly cautioned to do so. If no such permission is obtained by the licensee, then the licensee must use only original music and materials that the licensee owns and controls. Licensees are solely responsible and liable for clearances of all third-party copyrighted materials, including without limitation music, and shall indemnify the copyright owners of the play(s) and their licensing agent, Concord Theatricals Corp., against any costs, expenses, losses and liabilities arising from the use of such copyrighted third-party materials by licensees. For music, please contact the appropriate music licensing authority in your territory for the rights to any incidental music.

IMPORTANT BILLING AND CREDIT REQUIREMENTS

If you have obtained performance rights to this title, please refer to your licensing agreement for important billing and credit requirements.

www.ingramcontent.com/pod-product-compliance
Lightning Source LLC
Chambersburg PA
CBHW072018290426
44109CB00018B/2273